Best
Practices
for
Effective
Boards

E. LeBron Fairbanks
Dwight M. Gunter II
James R. Couchenour

BEACON HILL PRESS
OF KANSAS CITY

Cover Design: J.R. Caines
Interior Design: Sharon Page

All Scripture quotations not otherwise designated are from *The Holy Bible New
International Version*® (NIV®). Copyright © 1973, 1978, 1984, 2011 by Biblica, Inc.™
Used by permission. All rights reserved worldwide.

Scripture quotations marked KJV are from the King James Version of the Bible.

Library of Congress Cataloging-in-Publication Data

Gunter, Dwight M., 1960-
    Best practices for effective boards / Dwight M. Gunter II, James R. Couchenour, E. LeBron
Fairbanks.
        p. cm.
    ISBN 978-0-8341-2834-7 (pbk.)
    1. Church management. 2. Boards of directors. 3. Church leadership. I. Couchenour, James R.
II. Fairbanks, E. LeBron, 1942- III. Title.
    BV652.G86 2012
    254—dc23

                                                                        2012005336

10 9 8 7 6 5 4 3 2 1

Contents

Introduction

It goes without saying that the relationship of the leader to the board—and the board to the leader—has a tremendous impact on the organization's ability to fulfill its mission. That relationship also impacts the contentment, longevity, and success of the leader as well as the retention and longevity of the members of the board.

So how do organizations develop and nurture that relationship? What can be done to make the board on which you serve more effective, and the organization you serve successful?

As you pick up this book, you may be coming from a very difficult board meeting—the kind of meeting that makes you unsure you'll survive much longer as a leader or board member or that you even want to. You might even question the future existence of the organization itself. Perhaps you are preparing to meet with a new board as its leader for the first time or as a new director or trustee, and you are filled with excitement, optimism, yet a hesitant trepidation.

On the other hand, perhaps the board you lead or are associated with is doing well; you perceive nothing is wrong, but you believe it could be better. In any case, this book will guide you as a leader or member of a governing board in developing a stronger and more effective board—for the local church, for a not-for-profit organization, or for a higher education institution.

In the beginning, the prospect of writing a resource book comprehensive enough to be used by local churches, not-for-profit organizations, and higher education governance boards seemed completely impossible. The writers raised the question "Is there enough cross-over between these three organizational structures to write a cohesive book?"

After a half-day of discussion, we began to identify twelve best practices that were shared in common by all three types of governing boards, which later became the essential concept of each chapter of *Best Practices for Effective Boards.*

By the end of the day the writers of this book, Dwight Gunter as local church pastor, James Couchenour as not-for-profit organization board member, and LeBron Fairbanks as former president of a higher education institution, had begun to envision the development of a single resource for leaders and board members of these types of organizations. Not only do the writers of this resource book each have decades of experience working with boards, but we have also each been intentional about studying, writing, and systematically developing the boards we work with to create the most effective, strong, and healthy boards possible to serve the organizations we lead. It is our intention to pass this knowledge and experiences on to a generation of new leaders.

Each chapter, written by one of the three writers, represents a best practice for effective governing boards. The chapters provide a brief overview of the best practice and its relationship to board development. At the end of each chapter is an application section with some practical advice on how that particular best practice can be implemented in the local church, not-for-profit, or higher education setting. The application sections are written by specialization. While the applications were written to a specific organizational type, there are resources within the applications and appendixes that may be applicable to all three types of target organizations.

Join this journey of exploring the best practices of strong and effective boards. Then accept the challenge of this team of leaders to set aside a portion of each board meeting for a time of intentional board development. These best practices have been arranged in a progressive order guiding the reader from a solid starting point of development by establishing role, purpose, and function of the board to knowing and communicating the organization's mission, vision, and values. Next, the authors help boards ask the right questions and establish policy by establishing and maintaining a manual for effective and efficient governance.

As representatives of Christ and His kingdom, board members and leaders are reminded by the authors to conduct business in an ethical and kind manner—especially when they address conflict situations—and then speak to leadership and constituency with one voice. Board members intentionally and routinely engage in mutual accountability, communication, evaluations, and board development while taking the necessary time to process decisions, eliminating unnecessary surprises. Boards unite and resolve to work together through change and transitions for the good of the Kingdom, the advance of the gospel, and the prosperity of the organization.

Even though embracing the future, the authors remind us that boards are not afraid to assess the effectiveness of past decisions and collectively make appropriate, mid-course adjustments. Finally, the authors challenge us to exhibit generosity as board members and to be outstanding examples of giving regularly and sacrificially to the church, college, or organizations they serve in order to establish a culture of board development that embraces the principle of "passing it on" by developing new board participants, leading to a strong and healthy future for the organization.

In this volume are the collected wisdom and experience of decades of board leadership by three servant-leaders who have struggled through issues of frustration and bewilderment with board relationship challenges and the year-by-year journey of organizations attempting to survive in an ever-changing and challenging world. With this well-researched tool, these easily grasped and accessible principles can take your present board environment and develop it into an effective, efficient, functioning board to the health and success of your organization and to the honor of His kingdom and to the glory of God.

1
"Ears In, Fingers Out"
Dwight Gunter

Best Practice: Board members understand the role, purpose, and function of the board.

It was the getting-to-know-you stage of the pastor-church board relationship, and it was the April board meeting, my first at Trevecca Community Church in Nashville, as my tenure as pastor had just begun April 1. In this first official meeting I recognized this stage of the leader-governance board relationship to be crucial. I was sure they had questions for me, and I knew I had some for them.

Of the many issues we would eventually address, there was one imperative for us: we had to be on the same page regarding *purpose*. What was the purpose of the church board from the perspective of the board? Did their perspective mesh with mine? Did they agree with each other regarding the purpose of the board? Were we operating from the same playbook? Did we share the same expectations?

The answers to these questions are vital to the relationship between pastor and church board. In fact, the same truth applies to the leader of any organization and the governance board of that organization. If leader and board are not in agreement on the fundamental issue of purpose, conflicts will arise.

When the leader and board have different understandings on the purpose of the board, several dangers emerge. First, the board may focus on the *wrong target*. The board should concentrate on mission, vision, values, and policy. It should be looking forward, outward, externally, giving attention to the mission of the organization, thus empowering the accomplishment of the mission. To state the obvious, if the board focuses on the wrong target, the right target is missed. The result is the "well intentioned in full pursuit of the irrelevant" (Carver, *Boards That Make a Difference,* p. 19).

Second, if the board and leader are not in like mind regarding the purpose of the board, they run the risk of *differing expectations.* Unmet expectations form the soil from which frustration and anger spring up. Too many relationships between leaders and governance boards end in conflict due to this very issue—unmet expectations. Most often the cause of unmet expectations is simply a failure to clarify them. Note that even when clarifying expectations there is the danger of not living up to them, but that is another issue. A leader and a board cannot live up to expectations that have not been clarified—or if they do, it is simply a haphazard occurrence.

Third, *power struggles* often result. Who is going to make the decisions regarding administrative issues, such as hiring administrative assistants or terminating ineffective personnel? Who is responsible for the day-to-day operation of the organization? Financial issues such as paying the bills, producing finance reports, or monitoring budgets often become power struggles. These power struggles can arise in a variety of areas, depending on the size and scope of the organization—hiring faculty, setting operational goals, approving vacation requests, setting office hours, managing paid and volunteer staff, determining equipment priorities. You name it, and it is a potential power struggle.

Power struggles tend to center on the issue of control. When control becomes the goal, a true biblical understanding of roles within the organization is lost. People then take ownership in the church or organization in a self-centered way, acting as if it belongs to them instead of Jesus Christ. When the leader and board operate from the same playbook regarding the purpose of the board, power struggles are avoided, and the full leadership team operates as a body, with each member fulfilling his or her role with clear, well-defined expectations.

In order to avoid the dangers above and to help the board be as effective as possible, it is good to routinely remind each other of the purpose for the board's existence and the roles of both the leader and the board. I do this at the beginning of every new fiscal year.

Why is a governance board necessary? What is the purpose of the governance board? Most organizations have an organizational manual of sorts, whether a constitution, bylaws, or charter. Usually the purpose and duties of the governance board are delineated there. However, on a macro level there are excellent reasons for the existence of the governance board.

First, the board's foremost task is to *clarify mission*. If the mission of the organization has not been clearly articulated, then it is the responsibility of the board and leader to clarify that mission. This may take the form of writing a completely new mission statement, or it may involve a simple edit of an existing statement. Whatever the case, clarifying the mission is the top priority of a board.

Second, once the mission has been clarified, it becomes incumbent upon the board to *hold the organization accountable to that mission*. This is where many organizations falter. After spending hours and months developing and articulating a mission statement, the board and leaders often check it off the to-do list, cast it to the side, and lose it in the pile of projects considered to be the next best thing. Many times the next best thing has nothing to do with the stated mission.

Once the mission is clarified the most important task of the leader and of the governance board is to hold each other and the organization accountable to that mission. Every task the organization does, every decision it makes, and every resource it utilizes must be done with the sole purpose of accomplishing the mission. That is what it means to be missional.

Third, *values* are to be determined by the governance board. What do we value? What should we value? The answers to these questions are not always the same. Yet reality must align with intentionality. It is the role of the governance board to both define the values and hold the organization accountable to the values. For example, imagine one of the values of a local church to be grace. You can't argue with that. Imagine a social outcast visiting the church and desiring to unite with that congregation. Imagine someone saying to the pastor, "What is that person doing here? We don't want those people in our church." Does the value of grace shape the response to the misguided parishioner? Will the board take a stand for the values it has identified and committed to? It is the role of the pastor and board to hold the church accountable to the values, even if the implementation of those values is not always convenient.

Fourth, the board needs to be the arena in which *vision* is heard, shaped, synergized, and empowered. People often think of seeing a vision. That would make sense. But in reality, a vision is heard. As the leaders listen to the voice of God around them, they will begin to hear—and then see—the vision. God will speak the vision through people, circumstances, and the Word. The leadership must develop ears to hear the vision of God as He speaks it into the world. No wonder Jesus was constantly saying, "If anyone has ears to hear, let him hear" (Mark 4:23).

As discussion occurs regarding the vision being heard; then the vision begins to take shape. There is a synergy that develops as various components of the vision begin to emerge. Think of an orchestra with various instruments joining the music and the beauty that emanates from such a synergistic force. Direction can be established and the score written to accomplish the vision God is playing in the world. The board must then empower the vision to be accomplished. This involves finance, personnel, and so on.

Fifth, it is the role of the board to *determine policy*. The board becomes the clearinghouse for all policy of the organization. Policies become the tracks on which the organizational train runs. The policies are the parameters in which the organization functions. It is the duty of the board to determine these policies and implement them.

Sixth, the board has a *fiduciary* responsibility as well. The word "fiduciary" comes from the Latin *fiducia,* meaning *trust,* "a person . . . who has the power and obligation to act for another . . . under circumstances which require total trust, good faith and honesty" (<http://dictionary.law.com>). Board responsibilities include financial oversight. This requires integrity and faithfulness in all matters. Conflicts of interest must be avoided. The interests of the organization supersede personal interests.

Seventh, the board is also to determine the *general structure* of the organization. Even though there may be pre-existing parameters for the organizational structure, there is often flexibility in many specifics. The board is to set the structure in place and to do so with the mission in mind. Ideally a structure would be developed that would empower the accomplishment of the mission of the organization.

Eighth, the board should *give permission* for missional ministry to happen. Think of *per-mission.* Giving permission is allowing people to minister according to the mission of the organization. If the board tries to control every ministry in detail, it will fall into the traps mentioned earlier in this chapter However, if the board gives permission for ministry to occur, positive outcomes most often result.

The board can take several actions that will help facilitate a permission-giving organization.

1. The board should communicate the expectation that the ministry is to be effective. In other words, the board is not just giving permission but is hoping, praying, and expecting the ministry to be effective in the mission.

2. The board should provide clear budgetary and ethical guidelines for the ministry. These are most often articulated in the policy manual.

3. The board should leave the details of those ministries to the responsible teams within the organization. Let the team charged

with the task of leading the specific ministry direct the details in agreement with the policy.

4. The board can communicate a climate in which it is safe to fail. Without the safety to fail, risks will not be taken. The thinking might be "Give it a try. If we fail, we'll do something else." The results will most often exceed expectations.

Ninth, the board needs to *lead rather than react*. Too much valuable meeting time is spent reacting to various problems rather than leading toward valuable potential. It is necessary at times to respond to problems, but the task of the board is to lead to a preferred future more so than to react to past problems. Leaders lead. If the leadership leads to the past, is the organization then walking in circles? The board and the pastor are charged with the task of leading the organization into God's vision of the future. *Lead rather than react.*

As my first meeting with the board unfolded, we discovered we were on the same page and operating with the same perspective. The relationship developed. Mission was clarified, and we held each other accountable to that mission. Values were articulated, and we began to live them out. Vision—God's vision—for the church emerged. Specific ministries were developed, people were empowered to serve, and the rest, as they say, is history.

Ears In, Fingers Out: Application

Local Church

To state the obvious, pastors are busy people. Because the pastor's job is never completed, the challenge is to find ways for the pastor to stay focused on the mission.

A pastor working alone cannot keep the church focused on the mission. The leadership must share that responsibility.

The process I have used for helping the leadership of a church work through the issues presented in this chapter is simple but very intentional.

Step One: Articulate and internalize the mission of the church. The purposes of the church board have been presented in this chapter. It is imperative that the mission of the church be clearly articulated and honestly internalized if the purposes are to be accomplished. Chapter 2 delves into the mission in greater detail. Once the mission has been addressed, the board is then in a position to gain better perspective on its purposes.

Step Two: Clarify values. Think of this step as a project—an exercise—that can help the board grow in its understanding of Christlikeness. It is really a simple process of identifying things that matter, such as grace, character, stewardship, compassion, holiness, evangelism, and so on. Ask the board: How does God desire people to describe the church?

Step Three: Assign a team to create a policy and procedure manual. Don't make the mistake of trying to reinvent the wheel. Many churches already have policy and procedure manuals, and most will be willing to share how those manuals were developed. However, resist the temptation simply to copy what another church did—even with the church's permission. Each local church should tailor-make its own. The policy and procedure manuals of other churches can give guidance on the issues that need to be addressed and even how they addressed them, but each local church needs its own.

Once the mission, values, and policies are in place, the stage is set for the board to do what the board should do. Again, concepts are presented in this chapter that should prove useful in the ongoing work of the church board.

Not-for-Profit Organization

Most not-for-profit organizations are borne out of a heartfelt desire, passion, or specific leading of the Holy Spirit of one person, or a small group of persons, to meet a specific need. The passion and personality of the leader alone may drive the organization for an extended time, perhaps even years. However, without a functioning board, the organization's growth is limited to the capacity of the founder. When the founder is no longer available, the ministry falters, and many times once-powerful ministries close their doors.

So for new and emerging not-for-profit organizations:

Step One: The leader or leaders must understand the value of a strong, functioning board of directors and decide to establish such a board. For organizations that already have a board, step one will provide ongoing board development, based on the nine responsibilities noted by Dwight in this chapter.

Step Two: Assemble an effective board. It is important to invite only persons who share the passion for the mission and whose competencies add to those of the leaders. Passion for the mission is far more important than narrow technical expertise, because the board's decisions will determine the future of the organization, and mission must drive those decisions. Persons with technical capabilities, such as insurance, legal, and accounting, who may not share the passion can be retained by the board for guidance in those areas on an as-needed basis.

Step Three: Fully understand the role and responsibilities of a governing board and its importance to the organization. The guidance of this book, especially the wisdom of this chapter's nine responsibilities of a board, provides a sound basis for forming or strengthening a not-for-profit board. It is also wise to seek input from board members of larger or more experienced not-for-profit organizations.

Step Four: Write a crystal-clear mission statement. The most fundamental and crucial responsibility for all not-for-profit boards, especially those of new and emerging organizations, is to establish clearly the organization's mission and commit it to writing in clear, precise language.

Step Five: Explore and put in writing the board's response to each of the remaining eight responsibilities noted in this chapter. These are major issues, so it is important to allow ample calendar and meeting time to consider each one thoroughly.

Higher Education

Max De Pree in his book *Called to Serve: Creating and Nurturing the Effective Volunteer Board* quotes Walter Wright, former president of Regents College: "A board holds the future and mission in trust" (p. 24). In other words, the boards of Christian colleges, universities, and seminaries are responsible for determining the philosophy, the values, and the policies of the institution consistent with the mission, vision, and strategy of the school. It is not the board's responsibility to develop a strategic plan for the organization; rather, it is its mandate to insure that such a plan exists. De Pree believes that "while the administration's leadership team should be thinking through the strategic planning, the board should review and question and bring its perspective to the scrutiny of such plans (p. 25).

His chapter "The Marks of an Effective Board" recently caught my attention again. He focuses on "effective boards" because he feels that "the chief responsibility of boards is to be effective on behalf of the organization" (p. 8). He hits hard at a poorly constructed board agenda and calls this list of events or subjects to be discussed "an exercise in random trivia" (p. 8). He believes that "if the board regularly composes a well-thought-out agenda, there will always be a north star."

De Pree's marks of an effective board, as outlined in one of the early letters to his friend, are as follows:

17

1. An effective board has a mission statement.
2. An effective board nurtures strong personal relationships.
3. An effective board stays in touch with its world (whatever its world is).
4. An effective board does very good planning.
5. An effective board gives itself competent and inspirational leadership.
6. An effective board works seriously at the growth, needs, and potential of its members.
7. An effective board provides to the institution wisdom, wealth, work, and witness.
8. An effective board is intimate with its responsibilities.
9. An effective board decides what it will measure and does it.
10. An effective board plans time for reflection.
11. An effective board says "thanks." (Used with permission.)

Although De Pree discussed the design of the board structure and the role of the chairperson, I was particularly interested in the four categories of things the board owes the school leader: mandate, trust, space, and care (p. 81ff). He feels that the board mandate to the leader should include a mission statement and a strategy, "both of which derive clearly from who we intend to be" (p. 82). Included in the leader's mandate are "the statement of expectation and a definition of what will be measured in his or her performance institutionally, professionally, and personally" (p. 82).

De Pree feels the board owes the leader of the organization "space" to become the school president or organization leader. He discussed the need for a "workable structure," setting agreed-upon priorities, "as well as working to involve the entire organization in understanding and adopting those priorities" (p. 86). The board should take a strong interest in the personal growth of the school or organization leader. By "care" for the leader, De Pree means that the board should express care for the needs of the leader's family for friendship, support, and love; "the kind of care that goes the extra mile . . . including the need for continuing education and development—especially the opportunity to be mentored—and the kind of care . . . that doesn't permit the person to work himself or herself to death" (pp. 87-88).

Which of the "marks" identified needs the most attention in your organization? What can you do about it during the next meeting?

2
Mission, Vision, and Values Drive Us
Jim Couchenour

Best Practice: Board members know, communicate, and make decisions in light of the organization's mission, vision, and values.

Its high noon in a small village in sweltering central Africa when Kijimi, an African boy of seven years, happily begins his first trek to the village well to draw life-sustaining water for his family. Kijimi's father, Meto, smiles broadly at his son's eager willingness to embark on this trip, a major responsibility of his young life.

Let's examine more closely what is happening here and note the similarities with your ministry organization.

First, our mythical young friend, Kijimi, has a clear *mission.* It is to bring water—vital, important, life-sustaining water—for his family, who desperately needs it to continue working in the field under the hot African sun.

Second, as he starts out on that mission, Kijimi has "heard" the *vision* from his father. Now he "sees" it in his mind's eye—a proud father and a grateful family happily receiving him as he joyfully presents cool water to them.

Third, though not fully realizing it, Kijimi will accomplish his mission and achieve the reality of his vision as he performs his assignment within a distinct set of *values.*

Kijimi's experience is not unlike that of every member of a governing board. Each board member is called to fulfill an important role as a part of the board. Mission, vision, and values are indispensable in fulfilling that role.

It is certainly a high honor to be asked to serve on the board of an organization in which you believe and be given the opportunity to influence its future. Margaret Mead is quoted as saying, "Never doubt that a small group of committed citizens can change the world. Indeed, it is the only thing that ever has."

Serving on a board is also a serious responsibility. To be a world-changer, a board member requires a solid foundation on which to build thoughts and actions. The organization's mission, vision, and values provide that foundation.

In fact, a board member's number-one characteristic—his or her highest priority—is to know, communicate, and make decisions in light of the organization's mission, vision, and values.

A board member knows the organization's *mission.*

A board member knows with complete clarity the organization's mission. The target must be clearly visible and right. "Mission is everything" (Andringa and Engstrom, *Nonprofit Board Answer Book*, p. 22).

An effective mission statement's "ends . . . refers to the effect an organization seeks to have on the world outside itself" (Carver, *Reinventing Your Board,* p. 135).

A board member knows the board is the guardian of the mission. The board safeguards the organization's identity. The board holds the mission in trust for the "moral owners" of the organization. For the board member, the mission is not only to be known—it is also to be owned.

Three key components of an effective mission statement's "ends" are as follows:

1. It states the *results* the organization intends to achieve. The mission is stated in terms of what is to be accomplished, not in terms of activities in which to be engaged. It clarifies what changes there are to be made in the lives of those the organization serves.

2. It states who—*for what recipients or group(s) of people*—the results are to be achieved. There are potentially several groups of persons who could benefit from the results the organization seeks to achieve. For example, a compassionate ministry organization seeking to ease poverty in Africa must decide what country, region, and perhaps even what city, town, or village will become its focus.

3. It states what the *cost* will be to achieve the desired results for this group(s) of people. Every organization works within certain financial boundaries. The cost factor directly impacts the priorities of the results and the groups for whom those results will be achieved. The mission statement is clear about what those priorities are (Carver, *Reinventing Your Board*, p. 135).

As a board member grasps the mission, the distinctiveness of the organization is comprehended, and how it differs from similar organizations is understood.

The board member then is driven by mission.

A board member knows the organization's *vision.*

A board member sees the organization's future. This is vital, for as each board member sees the vision, the vision guides, encourages, and inspires. As a wise man wrote, "Where there is no vision, the people perish" (Proverbs 29:18, KJV). It is also true that a clear and compelling vision brings life to the people.

Vision flows out of mission and moves forward in two directions:

1. The board member has a crystal-clear mind picture of what the recipients will receive as the mission is accomplished. Excitement builds as the vision for the recipients becomes clear.
2. The board member also sees what the organization itself will have become as the mission is achieved. Watching the organization grow also adds excitement, because as it grows stronger, more of the mission can be achieved.

A board member knows the *values* of the organization.

As the banks of a stream provide boundaries within which the water flows, the organization's values provide practical, ethical, and moral boundaries to guide the board member. So knowing the organization's values provides the borders within which a board member thinks, prays, makes decisions, and acts.

Hundreds of thousands of Christian churches and organizations exist today as expressions of the kingdom of God. Certain values are common to all of them. Those values are based on Jesus' twin commands "Love the Lord your God with all your heart and with all your soul and with all your mind and with all your strength" and "Love your neighbor as yourself" (Mark 12:30-31). We place extreme worth or value on loving God and loving neighbor.

However, within these all-encompassing values, each organization develops specific values unique to its mission and vision. For instance, a college or university values higher education. A church values discipleship. A compassionate ministry believes there are no "throwaway" persons. This doesn't mean a church or compassionate ministry isn't concerned about or doesn't value higher education—it just means it isn't their direct mission. The values a specific organization develops facilitate that organization's mission within the Kingdom.

Whatever the unique values of the organization are, a board member knows them intimately.

A board member *communicates* the mission, vision, and values.

A board member is eager to tell others about the organization. He or she understands the importance of positive communication to the organization's "world."

Of course, the three most important items for the board member to communicate are the organization's mission, vision, and values.

A board member knows the organization's mission, vision, and values cannot be repeated too often. The goal is to have them known, owned, and repeated.

Communication takes place in four arenas:

1. *Within the board member.* In a board member's "self-talk," he or she muses about the mission, vision, and values of the organization. He or she personally memorizes the organization's mission and vision and understands their context.

2. *Within the board.* A board member develops positive relationships within the board. As a culture of trust grows among board members, based on the organization's mission, vision, and values, the board is increasingly empowered to speak with one voice.

3. *Within the organization.* A board member may have contact with persons inside the organization. In all interactions with administrators, staff, volunteers, and others, a board member stresses the importance of the organization's mission, vision, and values.

4. *Outside the organization.* A board member is a natural connecting point for all constituencies outside the organization. Contacts with business associates, social acquaintances, donors, potential recipients of the mission, the organization's supporters, government officials, and others are important. In all these connections a board member clearly communicates the mission, vision, and values.

A board member *makes decisions* in light of the mission, vision, and values.

In its fiduciary responsibility for the spiritual, financial, and programmatic well-being of the organization, the board is required to make decisions across a wide spectrum. The issues involved flow out of the board's unique responsibilities. Suggested lists of those responsibilities have been generated specifically for local churches, universities, and not-for-profit organizations. The major issues include:

- Establishing the mission, vision, and values.
- Selecting, supporting, and evaluating the leader.
- Ensuring long-range and short-range planning is accomplished.
- Planning financial and human resources effectively.
- Ensuring legal and ethical integrity.
- Assessing board performance.
- Recruiting new board members.

The decisions flowing out of these responsibilities are many and varied and become the responsibility of the board. Each board member is a meaningful part of that decision-making process.

How does a board make these decisions? Only by the guidance of mission, vision, and values will board members walk through decision-making without stumbling. The light shed by mission, vision, and values illuminates the path of decision-making.

Decisions must be driven by mission, vision, and values.

So in making decisions, an effective board member—

1. Stays passionately focused on the mission, vision, and values of the organization. Doesn't wander off into "interesting" side issues.
2. Screens all decisions through the filter of the mission, vision, and values. He or she asks, *How will this decision advance our mission?*

3. Serves the entire organization. All pet programs or departments of the organization and all personal choices are cast aside as the board works within the big picture mission.

After establishing the mission, vision, and values, the next most crucial decision a board has the responsibility to make is the selection of the chief executive officer of the organization. The title may be "president," "pastor," or "executive director," but the roles and responsibilities of the chief executive officer are essentially the same. This person is designated leader of the organization. The ramifications of this decision will reverberate across years, perhaps decades, and across all constituency lines. So, this decision must be more discernment of the Holy Spirit's leading than mere human intellectual capacity. It must be driven by mission, vision, and values, never by politics, personality, gender, or personal appearance.

As Kijimi engages his mission of drawing water with a vivid vision of a smile of approval on his father's face, he is filled with joy for having been given the responsibility, and he values the opportunity given to him. The same is true for the board member who accepts responsibility and accomplishes it by being passionately committed to the mission, vision, and values of the organization.

Mission, Vision, and Values Drive Us: Application

Local Church

Andringa and Engstrom are right: "Mission is everything" (Andringa and Engstrom, *Nonprofit Board Answer Book,* p. 22). So how does the leadership of a local church develop mission? Following are excellent steps to accomplish this objective. Three questions will help frame the missional issue within the context of a local church.

First: What results is God looking for? The Bible has addressed this question through a variety of images and metaphors: healing, restoration, reconciliation, salvation, finding something lost, freedom, blessing, and so on. It *should* go without saying, but it is so easy for leaders in a local church to forget: *God determines the desired results.* After all, it is His Church, His world, His creation.

Second: Who is the target? Another way to ask this may be— Who is the direct object of God's love within your reach? To answer this, use the metaphors above.

- Who is broken and in need of healing?
- Who needs restoring?
- Whose relationships are shattered and need reconciling?
- Who is dying and needs saving?
- Who is lost?
- Who is in bondage?
- Who does God want to bless through you? (see Genesis 12).

These are direct objects of God's love to be shown through His people.

Third: How can we accomplish this in tangible, particular ways? In other words, what does mission look like in action? This is vision.

A component of the vision of Trevecca Community Church is to help people who were in the bondage of addiction realize their freedom and wholeness in Christ. The specifics involve operating a transitional housing ministry that is structured to promote real freedom and wholeness. As of this writing there are eight such houses, and the ninth is in the process of being secured.

Vision grows out of the ground of mission. Mission first. Vision next.

Not-for-Profit Organization

Being mission-driven is the lifeblood of every organization. One serious threat to missional living for the not-for-profit organization is "mission drift." It is a reality—indeed the bane—of the not-for-profit world. Mission drift happens a little at a time. You begin meeting a need. Peripheral needs arise, and you meet those needs. More needs come, additional ministries are added, and on and on it goes. Suppose money is in short supply—as usual—and funding shows up for a good but not core ministry. The temptation to chase the money is overwhelming. Off-mission ministries grow disproportionately. Eventually priorities are lost, secondary ministries take precedence, and precious assets are used up on ministries on the edge of or beyond the scope of the mission. A missional focus can be maintained and mission drift defeated by following four steps.

Step One: Be on the alert for mission drift. It is insidious but cancerous to the organization. It will try to ease its way into the thought processes of those leading the organization.

Step Two: Stay laser-beam focused on the reason God called the organization into existence—the *mission*! Avoid trending toward being all things to all people by following Jesus' example. Even though there were still more blind and leprous people in Palestine when He struggled up the hill to sacrifice himself in our place, He knew who He was, what He was called to do, and didn't try to do more than what the Father asked.

Step Three: Challenge every board member to know and be able to quickly articulate the mission and vision. Write the mission on all written organizational material. Include it on the agenda for every board meeting.

Step Four: Expose every decision to the light of the organization's stated mission, vision, and values. Evaluate every ministry opportunity, regardless of how worthy, to see if it fits within the mission. The missional yardstick is the only reliable measure.

Higher Education

William C. Crouthers, president emeritus of Roberts Wesleyan College in Rochester, New York, and current president of Presidential Leadership Associates, a consulting organization for higher education presidents and boards, discusses the differences between mission, vision, and values statements and documents:

A Mission Statement

A mission statement reveals the basic purposes of the organization. It is a statement about the organization's reasons for existing. A mission statement may grow out of discussions around the following six questions:

1. Who are we?
2. What are the basic social needs we exist to meet?
3. What do we do to respond to those needs?
4. How should we respond to our key stakeholders?
5. What is our philosophy, and what are our core values?
6. What makes us distinctive or unique?

The mission statement clarifies an organization's primary intentions. An organization is a means to an end; it is not the end in itself. In other words, an organization serves a greater purpose that is more important than the organization itself. A mission statement defines the organization's role, brings focus to activity, and eliminates ambiguity concerning its reason for being.

Vision

1. *Vision* is a "see" word. What might the organization look like ten years from now?
2. *Vision* suggests a future orientation—an image of the future, an end result.
3. *Vision* connotes a standard of excellence, an ideal that can be realized.

4. *Vision* has the quality of uniqueness. What in the future should make the organization singular and unequaled?

5. *Vision* is a mental image of a possible and desirable future state of the organization.

Vision evolves through questions such as the following:

1. If we could invent the future, what future would we invent for the organization?

2. What is the burning passion we would like to express through our work?

3. What could be the distinctive role or contribution of the organization in the world?

4. What is our collective agenda? What do we want to prove?

5. What is our destiny?

Values

Our values will tell us how we expect to travel to where we want to go. Then describe how we intend to operate as we pursue our vision. Governing values include the following:

1. The lines that we will not cross.

2. How we expect to regard our students, campus community, vendors, and so on.

3. How we want to behave toward each other.

Models

A vision statement should excite and increase commitment. Implicit in a vision statement, however, are a multiplicity of assumptions about the configuration of organizational characteristics considered necessary for accomplishing a given vision.

A good way to facilitate the envisioning process at the outset is to develop alternative models, that is, alternative configurations of the major variables supportive of alternative visions. What major variables should be included in these models?

Givens

The creation of a vision does not mean that everything is up for grabs. This is not zero-based planning. It will be helpful to identify those things that we consider to be constants, or givens.

During the last decade the governing board of Mount Vernon Nazarene University approved a vision statement from the university president, a statement that was forged from a six-month-long conversation with faculty, staff, students, alumni, and board members—

Mount Vernon Nazarene University: an academic community of faith, shaping Christ-like disciples and leaders for lifelong service and global impact.

The document, *For This We Stand: Values Underlying the Mount Vernon Nazarene University Faith Community,* is found in Appendix 1.

3

Think
Questions
LeBron Fairbanks

Best Practice: Board members ask the right questions.

This chapter builds on the assumption that outstanding boards shape great leaders and that outstanding leaders embrace strong boards. This assumption requires that both leader and board ask the right questions of each other.

For this assumption to work itself out in the leader/board relationship, Christian maturity and mutual respect are required. Christian convictions about leading and being led will be evidenced as the policy-shaping and decision-making process of governing boards is experienced; convictions such as these:

1. Speak gracefully: *Choose carefully the words you speak.*
2. Live gratefully: *Don't whine—be grateful.*
3. Listen intently: *Seek first to understand.*
4. Forgive freely: *Be proactive in extending forgiveness.*
5. Lead decisively and humbly: *Combine deep humility with fierce resolve.*
6. Care deeply: *Value people rather than power.*

7. Pray earnestly: *Pray for change in you even as you pray for change in others.*

Local churches and other Christian organizations expect and are deserving of members of the governing boards who are mature and deeply committed Christians who can engage each other on the board with penetrating questions about working together effectively as Christians and as a board—questions such as the following:

1. If "in Christ, all things are made new," then how does our relationship with Christ transform and convert the way we live and lead within this board?

2. How can we work together as a board so relationships are redemptive and a witness to unbelievers of the reconciling work of God in Christ?

3. In the midst of conflicting expectations and seemingly irreconcilable differences, what does it mean for the church governing board to lead in these conflicting situations with the mind of Christ?

It is possible that the very functions of boards can nurture transformative, redemptive, and reconciling relationships within and between board members.

Good Questions, Honest Questions, First Questions

"*What* do board members do?" "*How* do board members do what they do?" "How do board members *know* what they are *supposed* to do?" Members of various boards may answer these questions differently depending on the nature of the organization. Local church board members, for instance, respond to these questions differently than members of college boards or community not-for-profit boards. The first step in strengthening the governing boards on which the individuals serve is to know the responsibilities of the board members.

On a cross-country airplane trip a discussion ensued regarding not-for-profit governing boards. One participant in the conversation was reading a book on board development. The other was the chief training and development officer for a large insurance firm and an officer in the national governing board for training and development professionals. The senior officer was asked, "What is the *mission* of the professional governing board on which you serve? What is the *vision* for the organization? Is there a *strategic plan* for the national organization that has been approved by the governing board?"

A fascinating discussion pursued until the plane landed. She could not state the mission or define the vision for the organization— there was no strategic plan. She wanted a copy of the book on board development!

Board members know and communicate the mission, vision, and values of the church, school, or not-for-profit organization. They ask good questions that lead to strong policies and decision-making with a laser-beam commitment to the organization's mission, vision, and values.

Questions About the Responsibilities of the Board

Strong and effective boards think and work in the three modes of governance.

Responsibility 1: *Fiduciary.* This mode of governance deals with the stewardship of tangible and overall assets of the church or organization. Fiduciary responsibility includes oversight of the church or institutional finances and the approval of an annual operating budget. These concerns compel boards to establish policies for the raising of funds, distribution of funds raised, and money received for the organization. Is a realistic operating budget in place? Are resources used wisely? These are leadership questions.

Fiduciary responsibilities ensure that legal and financial integrity is maintained. Are the results monitored? Is due diligence pursued? College boards, for instance, exercise their fiduciary responsibility for the financial health, academic integrity of the college, and the spiritual well-being of the students who study and the employees who work at the school.

Responsibility 2: *Strategic.* The board does not have to develop a strategic plan for the church or organization. The strategic planning process may be pastor-led or staff-led or arise from a board committee. It is the board's responsibility, however, to ensure that a strategic plan is in place. This requires a close working relationship with the pastor, staff, congregation, and the board. How is the plan designed, communicated, and modified? Are we proactive and intentional in strategic planning? Does the operating budget reflect the priorities of the strategic plan adopted by the board?

Responsibility 3: *Representative.* This responsibility is rooted in the values, traditions, and beliefs of the local church, school, or organization. Problems are framed in light of the heritage of the institution. Does this program reflect the values of the denomination? How does this expenditure facilitate the making of Christlike disciples in our community? How is the ethos of the college communicated through the academic programs? Are the decisions violating the values of the college?

Board members are representatives in two ways. They bring issues from the body to the pastor, and they reinforce the mission and vision of the pastor and board to the people of the congregation.

Board members ask good questions that lead to strong fiduciary, strategic, and representative policies and decision-making with a resolute commitment to the school's mission, vision, and values.

"Sense-Making" and "Problem-Framing" Questions

Strong and effective board members focus on value-defining, forward-looking questions that address the legal, planning, and restorative concerns of the faith community for which the board is responsible. These questions help the board make sense of the issues before them and frame the problems in ways that bring focus and intentionality to the discussions.

Vision questions that help us identity and address issues and clarify the missional purpose of the local church are similar to a journalist's foundational questions for any report: who, what, where, when, and how. Asked another way, we probe these questions:

1. Who are we?

2. Where are we?

3. Where are we going?

4. What is our end goal?

5. How will we get there?

6. Why is it important to get there?

7. How will we know when we get there?

When national education boards and regional accrediting agencies visit colleges and universities to review and evaluate the institutions and/or specific academic program areas, they ask the right questions. Though asked differently by various evaluators, the questions revolve around these categories of inquiries:

1. **Mission Statement:** Does your school have a mission statement that is known, owned, and repeated? Is it the filter through which every policy and decision is screened? Is there overwhelming evidence of the connection between mission, policies, and programs?

2. **Resources:** Have you marshaled the resources to fulfill the mission? Do you have a balanced operating budget that is mission-driven? Are human and financial resources dedicated to mission-critical personnel and programs?

3. **Tracking and Assessment:** Are you accomplishing your mission? What is your product? What is the quality of students you produce?

4. **Sustaining Growth:** Are you going to marshal the resources to continue fulfilling your mission? Do you have a plan to sustain and develop the financial resources needed by the school to fulfill its mission?

Board members vigorously and sometimes vehemently discuss policy options and make decisions within the board meetings but then need to communicate board action outside board meetings with a unified voice.

Shape the board agenda as appropriate to receive committee reports. However, the board agenda should be developed intentionally by planning significant time during the meetings for regular, purposeful discussion of key questions. Some boards structure their meetings around three broad categories:

1. Items for dissemination
2. Items for discussion
3. Items for decision

With this model the items for discussion are each stated in the form of a question. This discipline helps focus the discussion on the real questions being considered.

Good questions can lead to a strong synergistic partnership between the board and the pastor, school leader, or organization leader. Board members vigorously discuss policy options and make decisions within board meetings and communicate board action outside board meetings with a unified voice. This kind of relationship is like a good marriage. It is based on mutual respect, trust, commitment, effective communication, and good questions asked both ways, questions like—

- How would you define the "ethos" of the organization?
- What are you thinking or dreaming about the organization?
- What did you learn of greatest value this year?
- What are you hearing that the administration needs to hear?
- What are your concerns as a Christian organization?
- What is success, given your mission, vision, and values? What outcome do you desire? What is the end goal?
- What should you be concerned about as a Christian organization?
- What's going on? What are your concerns about the organization?
- What do I need to do if I am to be more effective as your leader?
- What questions do you need to ask to better understand the overarching problems we face?

When you engage these questions or topics, boards are freed from non-substantive issues. The important questions are asked and thoughtfully, prayerfully, and honestly discussed. A stronger bond between pastor/leader and the church board is developed. There is less micro-management and more macro-management, more leading and less managing.

A fusion of thinking is the result. Both pastor and board are forthcoming. Both accept a greater measure of responsibility for the policy decisions of the church. The board meetings are more substantive and focused on the strategies needed for the mission and vision implementation as opposed to being dragged down by the drudgery of detail by just managing the organization.

New direction for the future is forged together as opposed to dwelling on the past. Solutions to the significant problems are honestly addressed, decisions made and then implemented. Resources are aligned. Action plans are created. Pastor and board are moving in the same direction. Both are energized.

Strategic Questions in Crisis Situations

Pragmatist, philosopher, and educator John Dewey proposed, "A problem well defined is a problem half solved." In other words, work to clarify the real problem or issue that is creating the misunderstanding. Crises sometimes arise within the life of a congregation. Asking good questions is essential for a crisis situation to be addressed properly, the relationships within the board to mature, and the work of the board to be effective. Strong leaders are not afraid of tough questions from the board and to the board during these times—questions that look back, evaluate the present, and anticipate the future.

Evaluate what happened.

1. What is the real issue? Too often we deal only with the symptoms.
2. What *is* the question?
3. What are the facts?
4. What best explains the recent increases or decreases in attendance? Finances? Congregational involvement?
5. How is this crisis helping our people develop spiritually?

Determine where you are presently.

1. What are your expectations?
2. What do you see as the major challenges to the church or organization during this crisis?
3. What are you doing that is no longer relevant that contributed to the crisis?
4. What is the outcome we seek from this crisis?
5. What is the big issue facing you in the near future as a result of this crisis?
6. What are the consequences if you are wrong?
7. What changes in your organization or programs should be considered?

Anticipate where you want to go.

1. What are the possible solutions to this crisis?
2. What have you learned about working—or not working—together?
3. What are you doing that is essential for the future of the local church or the organization?
4. What are you not doing that is fundamental to the future of the organization?
5. What needs to change?

Relational Questions to Ask

Let's probe more deeply. As you think of the people you work with on the board, which of them do you have the most difficulty accepting? What kinds of people are hardest for you to accept?

1. Why do you think this is so?
2. How do you think this makes God feel?
3. How do you think God sees that person or persons?
4. How does your response affect your own relationship to God?

Pastors, school leaders, and organization directors often work with their governing boards in the creative and growth-producing tension of holding to your *vision* for the future while holding just as firmly to the *realities* of the present, including board members who differ—and often collide—with the leader. In the process of working through this tension, the leader and the board can experience the transforming, redemptive, and reconciling work of God in their relationships. What a powerful witness to believers and not-yet-believers alike!

Reflect on these practical lessons as you work together on the board to "accept one another, then, just as Christ accepted you, in order to bring praise to God" (Romans 15:7).

1. Good and godly people often see things differently.
2. Many issues over which we experience conflict are culturally based and not a violation of Scripture.
3. Differences that divide us have the potential to alienate members of the Body of Christ and to impact negatively the actual and perceived work of God in our communities.
4. Acceptance of our brothers and sisters in Christ who differ with us is to love, respect, and honor them as God loves them.
5. Acceptance of others implies that we can learn from them.

The overarching question is this: How can we mature in Christlikeness and increasingly reflect an acceptance of others (Romans 15:7) within the community of faith we serve as we function with integrity and grace as a governing board?

Summary

This chapter began with some Christian convictions resolute in strong and effective boards. These convictions about the leader and the led are evidenced on governing boards as the policy-shaping and decision-making processes are experienced, convictions such as to—

1. *Speak gracefully.* Choose carefully the words you speak.
2. *Live gratefully.* Don't whine—be grateful.
3. *Listen intently.* Seek first to understand.
4. *Forgive freely.* Be proactive in extending forgiveness.
5. *Lead decisively.* Combine deep humility with fierce resolve.
6. *Care deeply.* Value people rather than power.
7. *Pray earnestly.* Pray for change in you even as you pray for change in others.

Think *questions.* Effective board members ask the right questions, not just any questions. The questions presented in this chapter are only models. Each board will shape the specific questions needed for a particular time and setting. Boards may not have immediate answers to the fiduciary, strategic, or representative challenges before them as a governing board. They must, however, have the *right questions.*

Think *Questions:* Application

Local Church

Asking the right questions is imperative when trying to find the right answers. Finding the right answers to the wrong questions is an exercise in futility.

One of the first questions raised is what board members are supposed to do. This question is critical to the effectiveness of a church board.

Every year I have an organizational board meeting, which is the first meeting of the board who will serve for the new fiscal year. This meeting is the opportunity to get started on the right foot in the right direction. The primary focus of this meeting is to present the parameters of the function of the board, that is, what we do and don't do.

Clearly stated expectations are extremely helpful. Many people find it frustrating to serve on church boards. I've even heard of churches in which serving on the board was viewed as a necessary evil. That should not be. Most, if not all, frustration comes from unmet expectations. Therefore, clarifying expectations up front can reduce frustrations and increase effectiveness and enjoyment of leadership.

Asking the right fiduciary questions is a major responsibility of the board.

1. Have we developed an intentional, thorough, all-inclusive budget for the year, leaving reasonable room for the unexpected?
2. Are we operating within our means?
3. Are the income projections on track?
4. Are expenses staying within the authorized budget?
5. Are obligations being paid? Denominational allocations? Debt service? Utilities? Salaries?
6. Are we appropriating funds for future vision?
7. Are we financially supporting the mission and vision, or are we keeping ineffective ministries on life support?

These questions, along with others, should be asked either by the board or by a subcommittee—finance team—that reports to the board. In either case, the board has the ultimate responsibility to ask these questions.

LeBron raised ten questions that are crucial to effectiveness. I ask many of these annually and some of these semi-annually. As I move forward in my role as pastor, I will intentionally ask all of them.

Not-For-Profit Organization

Asking questions, many questions, probing questions, is a neces-sary quality of the effective not-for-profit board member. Questions are asked to gain knowledge, facilitate reflection by others, and build relationships.

The groups of questions LeBron supplied in this chapter—First Questions, Board Responsibility Questions, Sense-Making and Prob-lem-Framing Questions, Strategic Questions in Crisis Situations, and Relational Questions—provide excellent guidance for the involved board member on what types of questions to ask the organization. A good sequence for the questions not-for-profit board members should ask is as follows:

First, "What is the board's role?" "What is my role?"

Second come the mission, vision, and value-defining questions: "What does the organization do?" "Why does it do it?" "How does it do what it does?" "Where is it going?" "How does it plan to get there?" "How will it know when it arrives?" and "Who is its moral owner?"

Third are the organization's strategic direction, program or min-istry effectiveness, the ethos of the organization, and the board's fi-duciary responsibility.

Fourth, asking supportive questions of the executive director, such as "How can I help?" "How are you doing?" and "Are we pro-viding the decisions you need?" creates a mutually beneficial bond between the board and executive director. The stronger the bond, the stronger the ministry.

However, in addition to these questions that are asked of the or-ganization, the effective not-for-profit board also asks its community what their perceived needs are. This can be asked directly of community leaders or through a community advisory board established by the not-for-profit organization.

Last, but in a sense most important, is asking questions of the recipients of the ministry, questions such as "Are we providing a benefit to you?" "Is there any other way we can help?" "Do you feel respected and valued by us?" Asked in a respectful, dignity-enhancing manner, these readily communicate that we believe everyone is of equal value and there are no "throw-away" persons. Listening carefully and sensitively to their responses will greatly enhance the fulfillment of the mission.

Higher Education

Leading Decisively with Christian Humility
A Leader Effectiveness Review Process
Higher Education Senior Administrators, Faculty, and/or Staff

In an attempt to be faithful stewards of the leadership assignment given education leaders, the following draft review process for each leader is provided. The term "leaders" is used to refer to the school president/principal/vice chancellor of a college, university, or seminary. The instrument may be modified for the school leader to use with administrators who serve with the school leader. Fundamental to the nature of this review process is mutual dialogue in response to good questions between the leader and the board of governors to whom the person being reviewed reports. This is a critical component of the review process.

The review has three sections. Sections one and three are to be completed by the school leader prior to the official leader effectiveness review meeting. Section two (see Appendix 2) is to be completed by the board of governors committee appointed to oversee the review process prior to the official review of the college, university, or seminary leader or the supervisor of the leader. The "Competency Grid" in section two may be used by the review committee chairperson or supervisor to facilitate the discussion of responses in section two.

The date for the review will be set by the committee chairperson in consultation with the school leader and review member participants. The committee chairperson will determine if a meeting of the review committee without the school leader is necessary. If so, the leader will be briefed regarding the executive session.

I. Reflections/Projections (to be answered by the school leader)

1. How does your specific assignment support the overarching mission and vis on of the institution you serve? Provide some examples.

2. Has your sense of calling and personal ministry been fulfilled through your leadership endeavors? If not, why? If so, how? Do you feel affirmed as a valuable asset? If not, why? If so, how?

3. In what ways have you developed and enhanced your job knowledge and performance? Have adequate opportunities been provided both for training and for personal growth since your last review/evaluation? Please give examples.

4. What specific tasks or accomplishments during the past four years best express your commitment to top-quality service and servant leadership to school constituents, including evangelism, discipleship training, leadership development, fiscal management, and vision-casting? How have your gifts and talents been most effectively used?

5. In what ways have your initiatives contributed to the numerical growth and spiritual development of the institution you serve? What additional resources might assist you as you strive to strengthen your school?

6. How can the climate of collaboration within the school and with other schools be enhanced?

7. In what ways can the board of governance support you to lead more effectively?

8. What are your three top institutional challenges for the next year? The next four years? What short-term and long-term goals have you established for your assignment in light of these challenges? How will you know when your goals have been reached?

9. Are your short-term and long-term goals aligned with the institution's strategic plan? Please give examples.

II. Leadership Behavior/Competency Grid (see Appendix 3)

III. Summary/Recommendations (to be completed by the college/university/seminary leader)

A. Provide a summary of your leadership strengths and how these are most effectively utilized in your ministry assignment as a school leader.

B. The ranking below is not an evaluation of past performance. Rather, it is a projection for the next four years. Rank in order of priority (1 = most important; 7 = least important) the leadership skills that should be nurtured during the next four years.

_____ Affirming and encouraging skills

_____ Asking and listening skills

_____ Conceptual and analytical skills

_____ Financial management and budget development skills

_____ Strengths, discernment, and delegation skills

_____ Networking and communication skills

_____ Timing and decision-making skills

C. Provide a summary of your leadership limitations and how you plan to address these during the next four years.

The complete Leader Effectiveness Review and Competency Grid are included in Appendix 2 and Appendix 3.

4

Write It Down

Jim Couchenour

Best Practice: Board members understand and embrace a board policy manual that contains the board-approved policies for effective and efficient governance of the organization.

Minnie, the lovable church mouse, upon hearing the board members gathering ran into the board room, as was her custom, and hid behind the corner table, eager to eavesdrop once again on the discussion. She enjoyed hearing the conversation but knew how it would proceed and even what the decisions would be, since she had overheard them every month for the last two years.

As Minnie watched and listened, we board members sat around the conference table looking at each other. It became a long meeting, and most of us were becoming tired. Miscellaneous items had been discussed in excruciating detail, seemingly interminably. Frustration and confusion were evident as another of the old issues was brought up once again. None of us remembered what was decided the last time. So another extended discussion ensued with everyone trying to remember what we decided and whether the circumstances were different. By this time even Minnie was becoming tired.

Sound familiar? Sometimes a board just listens to reports and nods agreement. At times a board becomes entangled in minutia. At other times a board can become bogged down dealing with the same old issues. Most board members remember meetings like this and have no desire to return to them.

Are boards doomed to function this way? Can this be avoided? Is there a better way? What can be done to reduce the likelihood of this scenario happening in your board? If there is a solution, what is the next step?

It is possible to avoid these scenarios if the board plans in advance how to approach its assignment. There are many ways for a board to organize its work wisely. One proven way is to develop a set of policies within which the board agrees to operate. As outlined in chapter 1, the first three responsibilities of the board are to define the mission, define the vision, and define the values. The fourth responsibility is to develop policies to implement action on the first three.

The fourth responsibility, the development of policies, can provide a logical framework within which the board can discharge its duties, thereby minimizing frustration and maximizing effectiveness. Creating a somewhat standard way of dealing with the issues it faces, the board can operate without redundancy of discussion and action. Carefully organized and crafted policies, flowing out of the articles of incorporation and the bylaws, answer in advance many of the questions and issues that come to the board.

One way to organize policies is to group them by subject. John Carver in his book *Boards That Make a Difference* identifies four major categories of policies. Each of the four describes one of the board's major functions. These policies can be shown, per Dr. Carver, as quadrants of a circle. They can also be listed sequentially as sections of a manual (p. 157ff).

Section One: Ends, which focuses on the mission, vision, and values, is the most important section. Here the board and administrative leadership define the "ends toward which the organization is dedicated," its mission and vision. As stated in the "best practices" in

48

chapters 1 and 2, establishing or reaffirming the organization's mission and vision is the board's most important assignment. In this section policies are developed that answer questions such as the following: For what reason does the organization exist? How will the world be improved by what we will do? Who will benefit from our existence? In what way(s) will they benefit? How will we prioritize what we do so that the maximum benefit is provided to the greatest number of persons needing these benefits? How much will it cost to provide these benefits? Because we are trustees of the organization, it is important that we ask for whom we hold this organization in trust. Who is our primary moral owner?

In determining our mission and vision, it is important to describe the outcomes we intend to produce rather than the programs or activities in which we intend to engage.

Attendant to the mission and vision is the clarifying of values unique to the organization's heritage and mission. Here we answer questions such as—What beliefs or values are important to guide us as we fulfill our mission? Are there ethical standards we want to uphold? Are there ways of living that we cherish? In accomplishing our mission and vision, are there by-products of doing our work for which we want to become known?

The remaining three sections are significantly different from the first. The first dealt with *ends.* These three describe the *means* through which the ends are to be achieved. This is much like a Christ-follower is committed to the end of knowing Christ and becoming like Him. It is through means of grace that the end is pursued. Although the means are necessary, they are not pursued as ends; rather, they facilitate the achieving of the ends. Let's look at the three *means* sections (p. 160).

Section Two: Executive Limitations defines and describes the parameters the board sets within which the CEO will operate in accomplishing the organization's mission. These boundaries provide guidance to the CEO regarding what the board believes to be important. These boundaries may be stated in negative terms, such as "the CEO shall not fail to treat every person with respect and dignity." The advantage of using negative terms actually frees the CEO to utilize his or her imagination to do anything that does not violate the stated parameters, without having to come back to the board for approval. Of course, the parameters can be stated in positive terms as well. The challenge is to be specific enough to provide complete clarity on what the board desires. Some of the issues to be addressed in this section include—

- Finances
- Personnel
- Programs
- Facilities
- Organizational image and reputation
- Annual corporate and personal goals (p. 163)

Section Three: Board-Executive Relationship describes the linkage between the board and the primary non-board component of the organization, that being the administrative team, and clarifies the board's philosophy regarding that linkage.

At this point a major decision needs to be made regarding that connection. Will the CEO alone be responsible to the board and be the sole connection of the board to the administrative team, or will other groups/members of the organization's team be involved, and if so, to what extent? Will the board carry total governance responsibility and delegate responsibility solely to the CEO, or will there be shared governance? If it is to be shared governance, what governance authority will the board delegate to the various entities within the non-board part of the organization? For instance, in a university setting, will the faculty be a governance partner? Or within the unique local church board mandates many congregations have (in which the pastor is a member of the board and also the chairman of the board), how will governance be shared? (p. 165).

Section Four: Board Process describes how the board will do its work. It describes the board's governing style. Will we be forward-looking in focus? Will we be value-defining? Will we be a governing board or a facilitating board?

Will we work within policies or randomly? How will we relate to each other? In the differing opinions, which will certainly come, will we have "rules of engagement" to follow? Will we be autocratic or democratic? What committees are needed to accomplish our work? What principles will guide our committee work? What is the chairperson's role? What is expected from each board member? Should we have a code of conduct for each board member? If so, what should it include? (p. 166).

How are effective policies created? To avoid a strong "top down" authoritarian organization, we believe it is best for the board and administration to collaborate in developing the board's policies. This is especially important when policy governance is being developed for an existing organization. Participation from the CEO and the board in the development of policies creates an environment conducive to cooperation when the policies are implemented.

The goal is to develop policies that, when interpreted by reasonable persons, will accomplish what the board desires. On certain issues one policy statement may suffice while other issues may require several statements. Dr. Carver suggests using the "nesting bowl" principle when developing policies. In the kitchen, larger bowls have progressively smaller bowls placed within them. So in developing policies for any given issue it is best to begin with the broadest possible statement pertaining to the issue, then develop progressively narrower statements until the degree of specificity desired by the board is reached.

Write them down! Once the policies are developed, it is extremely important to put them in writing, place them in a board standing policy manual (BSPM), and provide each board member with a copy for continuous reference. The benefits of a BSPM include the following:

- Efficiency of having all ongoing policies in one place.
- Ability to quickly orient new board members to current policies.
- Elimination of redundant or conflicting policies.
- Ease of reviewing current policies when considering new issues.
- Clear, proactive policies to guide the CEO and staff.

Write It Down: Application

Local Church

Within the framework of a local church it is crucial to develop and maintain a policy and procedure manual. Let's talk local church.

We develop and maintain our policies and procedures through our personnel and parish ministry action team (P&P MAT). It is part of the annual work of the P&P MAT to review all policies and recommend to the church board any modifications, additions, and deletions as necessary. The board accepts, rejects, or modifies the recommendations. If the modification is too drastic, the recommendation goes back to the P&P MAT for further work.

One note of caution: develop only policies that are necessary. Don't create policies just to do it. "Simple, concise, and absolutely necessary" should be the rule of thumb. Remember: this is a legal document, and law will hold the local church accountable to it.

As I suggested in my response in chapter one, don't feel the pressure to create from *ex nihilo.* There are many good resources available to guide the process of creating a policy and procedure manual. Other churches will be of help as well.

Not-for-Profit Organization

Many not-for-profit organizations are the first of their kind, and there is no history or road map for the board to follow. Often the founding board, if indeed there was one, was comprised of friends of the leader(s). When this occurs, the tendency is for the board to be a "following" board, following the founding leader's guidance essentially without question. As the organization grows, systems and procedures are needed, and the value of board development becomes apparent. At this point, to properly serve the organization and the Kingdom, the effective not-for-profit board and leader must work together to organize the board for governance and consistent decision-making. To accomplish this, three basic steps are required.

Step One: Develop a set of policies within which to operate to achieve the mission. The goal is to delineate the roles, responsibilities, and relationships of the leader and the board, thereby creating a strong partnership—a shared-governance between the leader and the board. The subject matter of the policies can be arranged as listed in this chapter: ends, executive limitations, board-executive relationship, and board process.

Step Two: Place the policies in a board standing policies manual (BSPM), and provide a personal copy to each board member. Unwritten policies tend to be forgotten over time. A written BSPM, always available for continuous reference, eliminates the confusion brought on by forgotten policies. It also allows new board members to get up to speed quickly.

Adapt the template in Appendix 4, which was created for a university, as the template for your not-for-profit organization. It is wise to limit the number of policies to only what is necessary to accomplish the goals of the organization.

Step Three: Appoint a board development committee to keep the BSPM current and facilitate overall board development as well. This committee can also create an effective orientation process for new board members.

Higher Education

One seminary outside North America used the following template to develop its BSPM. Of course, school leaders and boards modify and adapt the template as needed and begin to include the key material necessary for the four major policy sections referenced in the chapter and below. See Appendix 4 for a draft of the BSPM developed by a university in North America.

Draft Template for Board Standing Policies Manual
Insert Name of Institution
Country
Date
A forward-looking, value-defining, and facilitating board.

Introduction

This board standing policies manual contains all the standing or ongoing policies adopted by the Board of Trustees.

Reasons for Adoption

The reasons for adopting this evolving manual include the following—

1. Efficiency of having all ongoing board policies in one place.
2. Ability to quickly orient new board members to current policies.
3. Elimination of redundant or conflicting policies over time.
4. Ease of reviewing current policy when considering new issues.
5. Clear, proactive policies to guide the seminary president.
6. Modeling of an approach to governance that sister institutions may use.

Consistency

Each policy is consistent with the seminary bylaws and the implementing rules and regulations, which have precedence over this board policy document. The school president will be held accountable for developing all other institutional policies and procedures to be consistent with this manual.

Changes

Changes to this manual are possible at every board meeting. Except for time-limited or procedural-only policies (approval of minutes, election of officers, and so on), which are recorded in regular board minutes, all new standing policies approved by the full board will be included in this manual. Recommendations may come from any board committee or the president.

Specificity

Each new policy will be drafted to fit within the most logical policy section listed below. Each set of policies is drafted from the "outside in," meaning the broadest policy statement will be drafted first, then the next broadest, and so on. At this point in detailing each policy section, the board has stopped and essentially is saying, "We are now willing for the appropriate leaders to give reasonable interpretation to our board policy. Over time, the board can reduce or add to the specificity of its policies."

Maintenance of Policies

The board secretary will oversee the recording and publication of these standing policies. The president's administrative assistant will maintain the policies on computer and provide updated copies to the board when revisions occur. This manual is not likely to exceed fifteen or twenty pages. It may be amended to some extent at every board meeting.

Major Policy Sections
Ends toward which we are working—mission, vision, values

This section defines why we exist, for whom we exist, what we intend to contribute to those for whom we exist, and the priorities we assign to the benefits we provide to them.

I. Board Governance Process

This section defines how the board will go about doing its work of governing the organization.

II. Board/President Linkage

This section defines how the board will delegate authority and responsibility to the president.

III. Executive Parameters

This section defines the parameters/limitations within which the president will work in accomplishing the task assigned to him or her.

If you think this process takes too long, think of the time spent by Minnie in the chapter four narrative! It is best to delegate the drafting of the board standing policy manual to a small committee of the board in whom the full board has confidence. The committee will bring back to the board drafts of the sections on which it has worked for feedback and revision. The board may choose to work with a consultant to assist the board in the development of this important document.

5

Watch Your Words

LeBron Fairbanks

Best Practice: Board members communicate with each other and address conflict situations as Christians.

United States military leader General Norman Schwarzkopf stated, "Leaders need two things—character and strategy. If you can do only one, drop strategy."

Character counts. It really counts! The words we speak, as well as the actions we take, especially in pressure situations, portray the character qualities that flow from deep within the heart and soul of a leader.

Leaders often experience pain as we hold tightly to a *vision* of the future while embracing just as firmly the *realities* of the present situation. This is especially true when good and godly people do not accept the vision we have for our ministry assignment. This pain is often felt most keen y for the pastor, college president, or community organization leader in board meetings in which the leader's vision and the members' reluctance collide.

In these situations, strong and effective boards watch their words.

The subject of our speech and the power of our words are addressed several times by Paul in the New Testament. Read Ephesians 4:1-3; 25-32. Paul encouraged members of the Body to use their speech for the help of others, for their building up as the occasion may offer (verse 29). In so doing, Satan will not get a foothold in our lives (verses 26-27).

In New Testament Perspective, Dialog Is a Sacrament

Our speech should be sacramental, or grace-giving. We are to converse with each other within the fellowship in such a way that our words become a vehicle and demonstration of the very grace of God. In all our conversations, use of language and subject matter needs to be such that the building up and edification is of highest priority for the purpose of ministering grace to the hearer.

For Paul, there is no room for words that degrade another person. "Do not let any unwholesome talk come out of your mouths" (Ephesians 4:29). "Let your conversation be always full of grace, seasoned with salt" (Colossians 4:6). Throughout the biblical narrative, the mouth is representative of the whole body and reveals the whole person. For Paul, one's speech reveals the quality of his or her relationship with Christ. Jesus said, "The mouth speaks what the heart is full of" (Matthew 12:34).

We are talking about not a technique but an attitude, ways of thinking and speaking to others that communicate—

I need you. (You have gifts and strengths that I don't have to affirm, disciple, correct, and build up.)

I love you. (You are my brother [sister] in Christ.)

I accept you. (You are being changed by Christ as I am being changed.)

I trust you. (You desire to serve the same Christ as I.)

I respect you. (You are different, yet we are one in Christ.)

I serve you. (I want to minister grace to you.)

Our speech must go beyond just being motivated by the right attitude—it also must have an intense, intentional focus on our situationally sensitive and relationally selective choice of words. Speak words that are "helpful in building others up according to their needs, that it may benefit those who listen" (Ephesians 4:29). There must be a focus beyond one's self, beyond self-serving comments and on the needs of the situation and those who will hear. Words spoken must focus—they must be on the building-up of others.

Our Words *Can* Be Destructive

Myron C. Madden states in his book *The Power to Bless* that "All who have influence and weight with others have the power to bless and to withhold blessing, to cause to grow or to wither, to help or to hinder, to heal or to hurt."

I (LeBron) listened recently by phone to a pastor friend who seemed to be in a state of shock and disbelief. He and his wife were enjoying their first pastorate after serving bi-vocationally in ministry for several years. But it turned out that his vision for the congregation was not accepted, and conflict on other issues emerged. Without being told by the board, his wife discovered that the family insurance payments were not paid, and at the same time the salary was being withheld. According to him, several board members started attending other churches.

Gratefully, he was able to secure his previous job, and his district superintendent placed him in a smaller church closer to his work. Board members, congregation, and parsonage family, individually and collectively, were stunned and hurt. The church's witness in the community suffered.

We do not know what went wrong in that pastor/board relationship. However, Sven Wahlroos in his book *Family Communication* discussed a series of "unfair communication techniques" used with families, techniques that may have been witnessed within board meetings mentioned above. Wahlroos discusses the "unfair communication techniques" of silence, ignoring, pouting, sarcasm, and ridicule (p. 123-190).

He also expresses concern over unfavorable comparison, exposing dirty linen in public, blaming the person for something he or she cannot help or can do nothing about, intimidating, yelling, exploding, bragging, nagging, and whining. That is quite a list! Yet it is quite easy to fall into the defensive and ineffective use of these unfair communication techniques.

When tempted to use words in destructive ways, consider the following questions:

- Will what I say build up or tear down the other person?
- Would I say what I am saying directly to the person involved?
- Do I know all the facts, or am I responding on the basis of half-truths or partial facts?
- Is my response triggered more by emotion than by reason? What is my motive, my intention, the real desire of my response? Is it self-centered or Christ-honoring?
- Is the issue really deserving of the attention and energy I am giving it?
- Have I tried to accept the feelings of the other person and understand why the other person feels the way he or she does?

Sometimes being emotionally honest requires criticism of another person in an appropriate manner. Wahlroos suggests that for every criticism of another person with whom we differ, we should find eight reasons to *praise* the person. This praise-to-criticism ratio can work in the home, at work, in the congregation, and during board meetings.

Words cannot be superficial. They must be honest. Use expressions such as *Thank you, I appreciate you, You were helpful,* and *I am grateful for you.*

Regarding conflict within the body of Christ, believers are challenged not to sin in their anger. "Do not let the sun go down while you are still angry, and do not give the devil a foothold" (Ephesians 4:26-27). Rather, Christians are instructed to be immediate and not delay in dealing with conflict. Delaying allows Satan to get a foothold in our lives—and into the congregation, the board, or any other fellowship.

The choice is ours. If we are intentional, our words can be filled with blessings, encouragement, and praise, giving honor and witness to the marvelous grace of God. Or, if we are not careful, our words can be destructive to the fellowship of faith and even tarnish the testimony of the church to our communities.

Our Speech Must Be Devotional (Spirit-inspired)

We grieve God when we tear others down and fail to deal with our conflict in a mature, Christlike manner (Ephesians 4:30) and in ways consistent with the Holiness testimony we profess.

Do Christian board members relate to their leader and to each other in ways that are no different from the ways non-Christians relate to each other in conflict? As Spirit-filled believers serving on boards, we have a fundamentally different mode of operation, and we function differently in relationships based on godly speech.

The Spirit of God is deeply concerned about the speech of His people. We are not to speak "unwholesome words." He instructs us to build up and encourage one another. Again, we grieve God when we tear others down and fail to deal with our conflict in ways consistent with the Holiness testimony we profess.

Ephesians 4 begins with the challenge to walk worthy of our calling as Christians. The characteristics of this challenge for the believer "walking worthy" follow. These guidelines instruct us to be gentle, humble, patient, and supportive of each other (verse 2) through "speaking the truth in love" (verse 15). Specific directions are given in verses 25 through 32 on how Christians are to speak truthfully in love to one another. Let us exam some of these principles.

Followers of Christ are to be co-laborers together in the Body of Christ (verse 25). The people with whom we work are God's own creation. Because of this fundamental Christian conviction, we can be *honest* with believers, *immediate* in dealing with conflict, *building others up* with our words, and *forgiving*, even when others do not forgive us. Words and deeds done by others to us must never be permitted to create bitterness and resentment within us. By the empowerment of the Holy Spirit we must guard our hearts and be holy in our responses.

When we ignore our "family" relationship in Christ and treat those with whom we work as a "means to an end," or to be manipulated for our purposes, Satan gets a foothold into the Christian community. The enemy of our soul laughs at unresolved conflict, which divides the fellowship of the faithful.

The resolution of conflict among Christians is an opportunity to bring glory and honor to God. Our words are to be channels of God's grace to others (Ephesians 4:30). God's forgiveness frees us to take the initiative in forgiving those who hurt us. When we do not live together by these guidelines as a Christian community, the Spirit of God is grieved (verse 30), and our collective witness to the world suffers. For more on the subject of conflict resolution, read "On Caring Enough to Confront" in Appendix 5.

In reviewing Ephesians 4:25-32, leaders see more clearly the means by which to "keep the unity of the Spirit through the bond of peace" (verse 3) and in so doing to walk (lead) worthy of our calling as leaders. Leaders translate their Holiness testimony to a lifestyle of wholly *leading*.

The opening verses of the following chapter (Ephesians 5:1-2) challenge us to "Follow God's example, therefore, as dearly loved children and walk in the way of love, just as Christ loved us and gave himself up for us as a fragrant offering and sacrifice to God." We can sacrificially live and *lead* with "[a life] of love, just as Christ loved us" through being "filled with the Spirit and speaking to one another with psalms, hymns, and songs from the Spirit. Sing and make music from your heart to the Lord, always giving thanks to God the Father for everything, in the name of our Lord Jesus Christ. Submit to one another out of reverence for Christ" (Ephesians 5:18-21).

Talking Past Each Other

A friend of mine once had a very vivid dream of traveling to an inner city and finding that he was witnessing a violent argument in a convenience store. He discovered that the argument was between a man from the inner city and another man, who was not from the inner city. Each side believed very intently in what he was passionately debating.

The startling conclusion of this revealing dream was the person from the inner city declaring to the outsider, "You will never understand—you are not from here."

As my friend told me of this experience, he said that he awoke from his dream and reflected upon what he experienced and the meaning of his dream. He said, "I really don't know who was right and who was wrong. I don't even know what should be done in a situation like this." He paused, then spoke with intense passion: "I really don't know who is right or wrong, but it seems that they were talking right past each other."

How often this scenario is played out in real life! How painful when it happens in local churches or college and community boards! Regardless of where we are or the perspective we bring to the board issue, board members must talk *to* each other. They seek first to understand. Members of strong and effective boards communicate with each other and address conflict situations as Christians.

"In him you too are being built together to become a dwelling in which God lives by his Spirit" (Ephesians 2:22). God the Holy Spirit is intensely interested in our "talking" and in our relationships. He will enable us to hear what we should hear, see what we should see, and speak what we should speak. If we believe our words spoken are of vital importance to him, then He can and will speak His very words through us. "Those who consider themselves religious and yet do not keep a tight rein on their tongues deceive themselves, and their religion is worthless. . . . But the wisdom that comes from heaven is first of all pure; then peace-loving, considerate, submissive, full of mercy and good fruit, impartial and sincere" (James 1:26; 3:17).

Summary

Henri Nouwen stated, "When the door of the steam bath is continually left open, the heat inside rapidly escapes through it."

Remember that the words we speak can bless or burn people. What comes out of my mouth reflects what is in my heart. Our words are to minister grace to others (Ephesians 4:29).

As Christians serving on the church or school board, supervising an employee on the job, or disciplining our children in the home, we either encourage or discourage, uplift or put down, speak positively or negatively, focus on the other person, or focus on self.

How do others feel when they leave your presence? Stronger or weaker? Larger or smaller about themselves? Confident or scared? Blessed or cursed? The Spirit of God is deeply concerned about the speech of His people.

In the book *Life Together: The Classic Exploration of Faith in Community*, Dietrich Bonheoffer lists seven expressions of ministry by which a Christian community must be judged and characterized. The first is "the ministry of holding one's tongue" (p. 92).

Bonheoffer paraphrases the book of James with these words: "He who holds his tongue in check controls both mind and body." He reminds us of the Ephesian 4:29 passage that admonishes us not to let any unwholesome talk come out of our mouths.

When these passages characterize us and define our relationships in decision-making situations, we bring healing and harmony by God's grace to difficult situations. We will be able to cease from constantly criticizing other people, judging them, condemning them, always attempting to put them in their particular places. We can allow others to exist as God's own creation, as brothers and sisters in Christ who are freed to serve as the graced, blessed, gifted, and called people of God! Amen!

Watch Your Words: Application

Local Church

Words matter. And in the context of a local church board, words have lasting effects—either positive or negative.

LeBron relates the strong truth that "dialogue is sacrament." How often have board meetings become opportunities for tearing down instead of building up? Speaking the truth—in love—is integral to effective leadership. Too often board meetings become a catalyst for *needing* more grace rather than being a *means* of grace. Speaking the truth and speaking the truth in love are not separate options. These are to be viewed as two sides of the same coin. Without both there is no sacramental dialogue.

To advance this goal I present and review two critical documents at the first meeting of the church board each fiscal year.

1. **Rules of the Road for Christlike Communication.** Another pastor, Charles Christian, introduced this to me years ago. He developed it to use with his church board. I've presented it every year since receiving it. The preventive effect has been wonderful. (See Appendix 6.)

2. **Rules of the Road for Christ-like Conflict Management.** This is a piece I developed as a result of a time of church conflict. Many of the concepts come from Norman Shawchuck and his work in conflict management. (See Appendix 7.)

By presenting and reviewing these documents each year, I lay the foundation for good communication and also for conflict management, should the need arise. I have had the privilege of working with church boards who took to heart these ways of leading together, and it has been sacramental to participate with them.

A phenomenon I've noticed over the years of serving as pastor is how at times a church will call a pastor and then view him or her as an enemy. To overstate the case, boards will select a pastor just to hate him or her. The same can be true of pastors. They go to a church to *fix* it rather than *love* it and *journey with* it.

I believe Ephesians 4 to be the greatest chapter in the New Testament on church leadership and operations. Paul makes a vital point by saying that pastors—along with other leaders in his list—are gifts to the Body of Christ. "He *gave* some, apostles; and some, prophets; and some, evangelists; and some, pastors and teachers; (Ephesians 4:11, KJV, emphasis added).

Lay leadership and clergy need to work from the perspective that each is a gift to the other. There should be mutual respect and value, modeling the way Christ sees us and works with us. A major component is our words. Watch your words.

Not-for-Profit Organization

Not-for-profit board members face the same communication issues as board members of Christian universities and local churches, but they also frequently encounter situations that extend well beyond denominational family boundaries, such as—

1. When other board members, though committed to the mission and vision of the organization, are from different theological traditions.

2. When board members of a Christian not-for-profit organization agree to serve on boards of community not-for-profit entities that are not Christ-based.

3. When not-for-profit board members have the opportunity or job requirement to interact significantly with local governments, judicial systems, businesses, and social agencies where opposing worldviews exist, the potential for conflict increases.

In these situations the wisdom of this chapter and its application sections are even more important. Our words must be carefully chosen to clarify rather than obscure Jesus for those who do not know Him.

One corporation has developed rules of engagement to facilitate effective communication. (See Appendix 8.) Other excellent tools are noted in this chapter and its application sections.

However, as David Augsburger states in his book *Caring Enough to Forgive,* "No relationship exists long without tensions. No community continues long without conflicts. No human interaction occurs without the possibilities of pain, injury, suffering, and alienation. . . . Without forgiveness, community is only possible where people are safely and cautiously superficial." Forgiveness, based on agape love as Augsburger describes it "results in renewed and reconciled community" (p. 6-7).

Some practical guidelines for the Christian not-for-profit board member:

1. Select and use the tool(s) best suited to your situation from Appendixes 5, 6, and 7.
2. Understand our words are as important to the Holy Spirit as to those with whom we interact.
3. Meet daily with the Father to keep the list short. Ask for guidance on every human interaction about which you feel uneasy.
4. Above all else, guard your heart, for speech, both verbal and body language, flows from the heart.
5. Commit to actively listen to the other person and strive to understand, then to be understood.
6. Make allowance for the huge difference between a pure heart and a mature character.
7. Offer true forgiveness, which flows out of agape love. (For more on this, read Augsburger's *Caring Enough to Forgive.*)

What a beautiful truth—dialogue as sacramental and grace giving!

Higher Education

Reference was made in this chapter to Sven Wahlroos and his book *Family Communication.* He states, "Make your communication as realistically positive as possible." As a guideline, he says that "the praise-to-criticism ratio should be kept at about 90-80 percent praise to 10-20 percent criticism" (p. 43).

Usually the opposite is true in our interactions with others. Sometimes being emotionally honest necessitates criticism of another in an appropriate manner. However, eighty to ninety-percent praise is needed (such as "Thank you," "I appreciate you," "You were helpful," "You affirmed me," "I am grateful for you."). It cannot be superficial. It cannot be syrupy, or it will be resented.

The issue is that the words we speak are to "build up others, according to their needs, that it may benefit those who listen." The focus of our words must go beyond ourselves, beyond self-serving comments. Our focus must be on the care and feeding of others, even in board meetings!

Some very personal and practical questions regarding the use of words emerge as we consider the Christian higher education community from the perspective of Ephesians 4:29.

Remember Paul's admonition: "Do not let any unwholesome talk come out of your mouths" (Ephesians 4:29). Corrupt talk is foul talk. Colossians 4:6 reads, "Let your conversation be always full of grace, seasoned with salt, so that you may know how to answer everyone." In biblical anthropology the mouth is representative of the whole body and reveals the whole person. In Matthew 12:34 Jesus said, "The mouth speaks what the heart is full of."

Back to the probing questions.

Do I tend to "bad-mouth"?

Do I tend to "shoot from the hip"?

Do I tend to respond quickly before I have all the facts?

Do I tend to talk about people behind their backs, saying things I would not say directly to them?

Do I tend to stress unimportant issues?

Do I tend to make excuses?

Do I tend to avoid reality questions?

Do I tend to use unfair communication techniques of silence, ignoring, sulking, pouting, cold-shoulder treatment? Do I use sarcasm and ridicule? Unfavorable comparisons? Exposing dirty linen in public?

Do I blame the person for something that he or she cannot help
or cannot do anything about?

Do I intimidate, yell, or explode? Brag? Nag? Whine?

These unfair communication techniques present problems with
what we say and problems with what we *don't* say.

Consider *these* questions regarding the use of our words within
the higher education faith community.

Does what I say build up or tear down the other person?

Would I say what I am saying directly to the person involved?

Do I know all the facts or am I responding on the basis of half-
truths or partial facts?

Is my response triggered more by emotion than by reason?

Is the issue really deserving of the action and energy that I am
giving it?

Can the situation be seen from a different perspective?

Have I tried to accept the feelings of the other person and understand why the person feels the way he or she does?

Paul is concerned with the role of words exchanged between individuals within the faith community. In the midst of mutual dialog
and the caring of the challenging business of higher education, God's
grace and power should flow through words used.

6
Strong Boards
Empower
Effective
Leaders

Jim Couchenour

Best Practice: Board members relate to their leaders and constituency with one voice.

The atmosphere in the room was cordial but tense. An issue of significant importance had arisen. The board had to make a decision—and make it now. It was the Board of General Superintendents of the Church of the Nazarene. All six members of the board gathered in a closed-door session to discuss the issue and decide what course to take. As the discussion progressed, most of the members seemed to be of one opinion. However, Charles Strickland, one of the newer board members, thought differently and strongly expressed his dissent with the opinion of the others.

After considerable debate, someone called for a vote. The vote was taken, and to Dr. Strickland's disappointment, the decision of the majority went against his opinion. Then the board chairman, to the surprise and dismay of Dr. Strickland, said, "Now that we've made our decision, I think we should appoint Charles to lead us in its implementation." So they did—and he did.

Although they had held different opinions during the discussion, after the decision was made, the Board of General Superintendents spoke with one voice. Quite some time later, as Dr. Strickland related the story, he told about the growth he experienced while implementing what he initially thought was not a good idea. One voice—what a wonderful compliment for any group to receive! One voice—it is not optional. Rather, it is imperative for a board.

A board is a unique entity. Margaret Mead, celebrated anthropologist, said, "Can a small group of people who see and respond differently to the world make a difference? Indeed, history shows that it is the only thing that ever has." This truism certainly applies to boards of Christian organizations. For a small group of people—the board—to *change their world*, each board member needs to know how to speak with one voice as a board. What does this mean, and to whom does the board speak?

The Board Speaks with One Voice

Each board member has a right and responsibility to express his or her personal voice on every matter with which the board grapples. Input from every thoughtful person is important. Expressing an opinion comes easily to some board members, while to others it may not be as natural. Even though you may be reticent to speak, the board needs to hear your thinking. The old adage "The group as a whole knows more than any one of the group" is true. Without everyone's input, the board cannot be all it is intended to be; every individual voice is required for the board to have a full voice. The board member and the board benefit greatly when everyone participates.

Good board members begin by listening to each other. Listening goes far beyond just hearing words. The goal is to actually understand what is being communicated. Though not easy, this kind of listening is imperative.

Good boards vigorously discuss policy options and make decisions within board meetings. It is important at times to express an opinion with passion—Christian passion—when the issue is important and passion is genuine. Always, however, board members strive to communicate compassionately, respectfully, directly, and supportively. God's guidance found in Ephesians 4:2, applies.

After the decision is made, board members communicate board action outside the board meeting with unified support. Many board members are chosen because they are self-starters. So for those board members the more difficult step lies beyond participating freely in the discussion. It is the challenge of putting personal feelings aside and in the end abiding by the board's final decision and participating in speaking with one unified voice as an entire board.

William Barclay in *The Daily Study Bible*, Volume 2, commenting on Jesus' prayer for unity of His disciples, writes, "He prayed that they might live not as units, but as a unity. Where there are divisions, where there is exclusiveness, where there is disunity and dispeace, the cause of Christianity is harmed and hindered, and the prayer of Jesus is frustrated" (p. 252). What is true for the Kingdom at large is certainly true for the board of a Christian organization. While maturity of Christian character is beyond the scope of this book, the basis for unity of a board is Christian love, which produces Christlike humility and true fellowship, which result in unity.

Christian humility and respect for others are at the heart of speaking with one voice. Genuine humility avoids sidebar discussions in the parking lot after the meeting, unchristian comments about fellow board members, and all other actions one can think of that tend to undermine decisions and leadership. Integrity matters.

Shared trust within the board is priceless. The ethos of an organization is a reflection of the heartbeat of the board. Therefore, it is incumbent upon the board to create a culture of trust. When a culture of trust is embedded within the board, it flows naturally outward in every relationship.

Board members intentionally engage in mutual accountability, including systematic board development and evaluation. Because of the importance of mutual trust and Christian communication, the board's ability to speak with one voice is included in the periodic evaluation of the board's own performance. True board development begins at this point.

Learning to speak with one voice inevitably strengthens and benefits each board member. In addition to facilitating personal spiritual formation, the individual board member experiences the joy of being one part of a meaningful whole and the gratification of participating in worthwhile achievements for the Kingdom. "Out of many one" is the goal.

The Board Speaks with One Voice to the President

A good board-and-president relationship is like a good marriage: it is based on mutual respect, trust, commitment, and effective communication. Indeed, the goal is to develop a synergistic relationship that enhances the performance of both.

The board and the president work together on a wide range of issues. They share in establishing or revisiting the organization's mission, vision, values, governance, strategic planning, and operational parameters. They work together to plan and set agendas and policies. They are a true partnership, two halves of one whole. A strong spirit of collaboration built on mutual trust, respect, and communication is vital.

An effective partnership begins with the board listening to the president and the president listening to the board. Mutual expectations are developed, and communication becomes a two-way street.

The president needs to be involved in any board development process, and the board must be kept abreast of major developments in the organization's areas of responsibility. The board is supportive of the president, and the president is supportive of the board. There is no undermining of either. The board depends on the president to carry out its policies, and the president relies on the board for policy guidance.

Board members relate to the president with one voice. Mixed signals from the board to the president about any aspect of the organization—current objectives, the strategic plan, a current or future specific issue—mires the organization in the quicksand of confusion and thwarts all meaningful progress. Activity may continue, but progress is halted. Gridlock freezes progress. A clear, unalloyed message from the board to the president is vital to the president's success and to the board's success as well. When the board speaks with one voice, the president, unconcerned about being shot down without warning, is freed to act with dispatch toward the achievement of the mission and vision of the organization.

Strong boards empower effective leaders; strong leaders embrace engaged boards. Few leaders of Christian organizations will be stronger or rise higher than their boards.

The Board Speaks with One Voice to the Constituency

Board members are usually elected or appointed by the constituency and in every case represent the constituency on the board. The organization's constituency is the organization's world. Individually and collectively, board members have the opportunity and responsibility to relate the organization to its world and its world to the organization. Board members serve as active extensions of the president and board to the constituency between board meetings.

Board members begin by listening to the constituency—listening to hear the thoughts and feelings behind the words. They appreciate the heritage and history of the organization. Understanding the past and listening to the constituency's current desires and goals assist the board member in fulfilling his or her responsibility.

Good boards speak with one voice to the constituency. Speaking with one voice demonstrates that harmony exists within the board. Mixed signals from the board send confusing messages. Speaking with one voice to the constituency strengthens the board/constituency relationship. All Christian organizations depend on the spiritual and financial support of the constituency as well as the all-important pool of future leaders. The truth is, the clearer the voice from the board, the stronger the constituency. The stronger the constituency, the stronger its support of the organization. The benefits of speaking with one voice travel full circle.

Summary

As mission, vision, and values are the filter for all board decisions, speaking with one voice is the filter for all the board's communication outside board meetings. The board's ethos is formed one conversation at a time. The spirit of the board and its culture are important. Speaking with one voice is an important piece of that culture. As a finished jigsaw puzzle with all the pieces in place reveals an integrated and complete picture, a board speaking with one voice to all its stakeholders reveals an integrated and complete board. In so doing, the board thereby also provides a model for other organizations and their board members to follow.

Strong Boards Empower Effective Leaders:
Application

Local Church

"The board speaks with one voice." What a crucial concept to the life of a local church! If the board does not speak with one voice, division will result.

One voice implies that the board as a whole must own the final decisions. There have been occasions when I as pastor was in the minority opinion of the board. The board voted, and I was on the losing side. So what did I do? When it came time to present the decision of the board, I acted as if I had voted for it. I *owned* the decision. The board functions as a team, as a unit, as a body. Therefore, when the body makes a decision and I'm part of the body, I own it.

Ken Blanchard and Sheldon Bowles make the case that "None of us is as smart as all of us" (Ken Blanchard and Sheldon Bowles, *High Five! The Magic of Working Together,* xi). If I insist on my own opinion, my individual perspective, or my personal desire, I will miss the benefit of the experiences and wisdom of the group. Blanchard and Bowles are right: none of us is as smart as all of us.

The church board must function as a team who empowers each other and empower the ministries of the local church. Trust is a major factor in empowering leaders. There are ways to increase the trust factor. I have done this through shared values, shared experiences, and shared goals.

I also increase the trust factor through the method of conducting the business of the board. Jim points out that "Good board members begin by listening to each other. Listening goes far beyond just hearing words." Some pastors are prone to get bogged down in the use of Robert's Rules of Order. The purpose of Robert's Rules of Order is to insure a courteous atmosphere in which fair communication can exist and group outcomes can be achieved. I don't bang a gavel. In fact, I don't even use one. As long as a courteous atmosphere exists, all can be heard. Hearing one another's heart increases trust and leads to empowerment.

Not-for-Profit Organization

A dynamically empowered, effective executive director leading proactively is vital to the success of a not-for-profit organization. The strong not-for-profit board recognizes this, takes the concern seriously, and makes the care, guidance, empowering, and appropriate evaluation of the executive director primary board responsibilities. A unified board *speaking with one voice* to the executive director is critical. The board must avoid sending conflicting signals. Any breach of this principle diminishes the effectiveness of the executive director and the board. The question is *How is the board to accomplish this?*

It begins with the board having the right ethos. *Merriam Webster's Collegiate Dictionary* defires ethos as "The distinguishing character, sentiment, moral nature, or guiding beliefs of a person, group, or institution." Every board creates and manages its own ethos. You have the opportunity to define the personality of your board.

The effective not-for-profit board creates and fosters an ethos including foundational beliefs such as inclusiveness, careful listening, humility, respect, trust, mutual accountability, function as a unit, a commitment to personal and board growth, cohesiveness, and *speaking with one voice.*

Chait, Holland, and Taylor in their book *Improving the Performance of Governing Boards* list "Six Competencies of Effective Boards" (p. 7). Competency number four is the interpersonal dimension. It deals with "developing the board as a working group . . . and fostering a sense of cohesiveness." To *speak with one voice*, a strong belief in and attention to cohesiveness must characterize the board. Cohesiveness comes from acting out the foundational beliefs in the day-to-day work of the board.

The result is when the executive director hears the board *speaking with one voice,* confusion evaporates, division is disarmed, and the organization can move on toward its vision. When the constituency hears the board and executive director *speaking with one voice,* support is enhanced in all directions.

Higher Education

Dietrich Bonhoeffer in *Life Together: The Classic Exploration of Faith in Community* lists seven expressions of ministry by which a Christian faith community (including its governing board) must be judged and characterized.

Seven expressions of ministry excerpted from pp. 91, 94, 97, 99, 100, 103, 108 from *Life Together* by Dietrich Bonhoeffer and translated by John Doberstein. English translation copyright © 1954 by Harper & Brothers, copyright renewed 1982 by Helen S. Doberstein. Reprinted by permission of HarperCollins Publishers.

1. The Ministry of Holding One's Tongue

"He who holds his tongue in check controls both mind and body," James tells us. "Do not let any unwholesome talk come out of your mouths" (Ephesians 4:29) is an admonishment from Paul. When this passage characterizes us, we will be able to cease from constantly criticizing the other person, judging and condemning him or her, putting the person in his or her particular place. We can allow the other to exist as a completely free person.

2. The Ministry of Meekness

Meekness is caring more for others than for oneself. "Do not think of yourself more highly than you ought," Paul tells us in Romans 12:3. John tells us to make no effort to obtain the praise that comes only from God. He who serves must learn to think first of others.

3. The Ministry of Listening

The first service that one owes to others in the fellowship consists of listening. Listening can be a greater service to people than speaking.

4. The Ministry of Active Helpfulness

Simply assist others within the Christian community in external matters, big and small.

5. The Ministry of Bearing (Supporting)

"Carry each other's burdens" is the challenge of Galatians 6:2. "Bearing" means forbearing and sustaining one another in love.

Ephesians 4:2 commands us to "be completely humble and gentle; be patient, bearing with one another in love."

6. The Ministry of Proclaiming

Proclaiming is the ministry of the Word of God. Bonhoeffer does not mean the message of Scripture proclaimed in a formal setting such as in the worship service. He is referring to the free communication of the Word of God from person to person. He is referring to that unique situation in which one person becomes a witness in human words to another, with Christian consolation.

7. The Ministry of Authority (Leadership)

Jesus states in Mark 10:43-44, "Whosoever wants to become great among you must be your servant, and whoever wants to be first must be slave of all." This is the paradox of ministry. Jesus made authority in the fellowship dependent upon brotherly service.

For Bonhoeffer, these practical expressions of Christian ministry provide the *context* that our specific ministries must function within. This is particularly true as it relates to the specific ministry of leadership in a faith community.

Christian leadership has been defined as "humble service to others for the purpose of enabling *them*, through teaching and example, to live *their* lives under the Lordship of Christ and to fulfill *their* ministry to each other and *their* mission in the world."

In applying this definition to board members of higher education institutions, it is appropriate to ask a follow-up question: "How can *my* ministry of Christian leadership on this board strengthen the school leader's ministry to others on campus and his or her mission beyond the campus walls?

Remember: strong boards empower effective leaders, and effective leaders embrace engaged boards.

7

Integrity Matters
LeBron Fairbanks

Best Practice: Board members intentionally engage in mutual accountability, including systematic board development and evaluation.

Jon Wallace, president of Azusa Pacific University in southern California, asked his board chair emeritus, Ted Engstrom, some questions. Dr. Wallace had just asked Dr. Engstrom a pointed question: "What do you want on your tombstone, and how do you want the first line of your obituary to read?" Without hesitation and with evident joy dancing in his eyes, Dr. Engstrom replied, "I simply want my tombstone to say, 'Here lies a man of integrity.'" He continued: "That's because the greatest hallmark for a Christian is to be known as a person of integrity . . . a consistency between our personal and public lives. A whole person. A complete person."

Integrity and Mutual Accountability

Integrity has been defined as honesty, consistency, and coherency—the same inside and outside. It is the number-one trait people want in leaders. It's what members of churches or companies assume they will receive from the boards that govern the organizations to which they belong.

Chapter 1 discussed key roles and responsibilities of boards, including fiduciary, strategic, and representative modes of thinking and functioning. Boards need members who are skilled in creative thinking, strategic planning, legal analyses, and community and government relations, as well as those who have an appreciation of the heritage and traditions of the organization. Boards suffer when they do not balance their time together with the appropriate attention given to each of these three modes of governance: fiduciary, strategic, and representative.

Periodic evaluation sessions provide the "mid-course" corrections necessary for the board to refocus and rebalance its energies on the mission, vision, and values of the organization. Assessing anew the context wherein we live and work, establishing growth goals, and developing implementing strategies reenergize board members as they focus on results, not just activity in board meetings.

Signs often warn a board that it is not functioning properly. For example, the board may spend too much time on trivial matters; the board meetings do not function from forward-looking and value-defining agendas; or members do not have the information they need on critical issues far enough in advance in order to think about these issues prior to the meetings. Another sign is in the insufficient time allocated during board meetings for discussion of critical issues facing the organization.

These and other signs may indicate that a board self-assessment is necessary, that it's time to pause and review the board's processes, procedures, and policies and to refocus the board on the mission of the organization. This self-assessment process communicates to the board and to the individuals whom they serve that integrity matters in the governance of the organization.

One option is for the board to choose to use self-assessment tools from BoardSource (<www.boardsource.org>). Another would be to utilize an objective, outside consultant. The executive committee or governance committee should lead the assessment and board development planning process.

Systematic Board Development

Effective boards are increasingly designating a certain amount of time in each meeting for board development. Where do the members need the most assistance in preparing them for the decision-making or policy-formulating issues before them? The designated time may be given to an emphasis on legal, financial, community, or denominational issues or concerns, or on the fundamental mission, vision, or values of the church, organization, or company. This expertise may come from within the board, congregation, community leaders, or national organizations via workshop, presentation, or video or videoconferencing. Board leaders should meet regularly—outside scheduled board meetings—with other board members to ask how the overall board is performing. Based on the assessments, the executive committee should create a plan for continuing board development.

A wise and effective chair will take the time for board members to tell each other what motivates them to serve. Board members need to be reminded why they joined the board and also receive affirmation and edification from the colleagues with whom they serve. Additional opportunities need to be provided to board members to increase their understanding of their specific roles and responsibilities on the board and within the organization. The chair should also provide occasions when "best practices" for governing boards are discussed and the current practices of the board are evaluated against that standard.

Regular opportunities to educate board members about the organization, its structure, and its history should be highlighted as stories and historical accounts are shared with them from the traditions of the organization. In order to move the organization into the future, not only is a firm knowledge and understanding of the history required, but also every effort must be made to educate board members about the current and active programs of the organization—especially their connection to the mission and anticipated future results and direction of the organization.

Board Development Questions

For college and university boards, questions such as the following may open the doors for subsequent discussions:

1. How does the work of the board support the overarching mission and vision of the university?

2. In what ways have the initiatives of the board contributed to the numerical growth and spiritual development of the university?

3. How can the climate of collaboration between the board, faculty, community, senate, and business leaders be enhanced?

What are the top three institutional challenges for the next year? What short-term and long-term goals have been established in light of these challenges?

Are the board's short-term and long-term goals aligned with the institution's strategic plan?

Other questions probe the level of satisfaction of working on the board, personal goals for working on the board, and how the overall board is performing:

1. How does your commitment and involvement on the board you serve support the overarching mission and vision of the institution, church, or organization? Provide some examples.

2. Has your love for Christ and sense of service to others been fulfilled through your endeavors on the board? If not, why? If so, how? Do you feel affirmed as a valuable asset on the board? If not, why? If so, how?

3. In what ways have you developed and enhanced your understanding of the roles and responsibilities of the board? Have adequate opportunities been provided, both for training and for personal growth, since you became a member of the board? Please give examples.

4. What specific tasks or accomplishments best express the board's commitment to high-quality service and servant leadership to church or school constituents, including evangelism, discipleship training, leadership development, fiscal management, and vision-casting? How have the gifts and talents of other board members been most effectively used?

5. In what ways have the initiatives of the board contributed to the numerical growth and spiritual development of the church or institution you serve? What additional resources might assist the board as you strive individually and collectively to strengthen your church, school, or organization?

6. How can the climate of collaboration, mutual trust, and intentional communication within the board and the church or school be enhanced?

7. In what ways can the board members support the church pastor, school leaders, and board chair more effectively?

8. What are your three top church or institutional challenges for the next year? The next four years? What short-term and long-term goals has the board established in light of these challenges? How will the board know when these goals have been reached?

9. In what ways did you contribute to the strategic plan for the church or organization you serve? When was the plan last reviewed and updated?

Board Survey

William Crouthers, Robert Wesleyan University president emeritus and president of Presidential Leadership Associates, prepared the survey in Appendix 9 for college and university boards to use in evaluating their effectiveness. This survey can be adapted for your local church board or community organization board as appropriate. If you are uncomfortable with this board survey instrument of Dr. Crouthers, then be intentional about locating a survey that is appropriate to your context or more readily adaptable.

Trustee Dashboard

A dashboard on your automobile provides essential information about the condition of your vehicle. With a glance you can know the amount of gasoline remaining in the tank, the adequacy of the water in the radiator, and the strength of your battery life. If problems arise with your engine, indicators are illuminated to indicate problems and to alert you that action needs to be taken soon.

Likewise, dashboard reports for governing boards provide a quick glance at essential indicators for the leadership of the school, church, or community organization. At a glance, if the dashboard report is appropriately designed for your board, you can analyze quickly the information you need to make necessary decisions. In creating your dashboard, establish appropriate benchmarks for essential areas. Too much data can overpower a board; too little information makes the report irrelevant.

Key dashboard indicators for local churches may include worship attendance, finances, discipleship classes, conversions, community outreach, and utilization of physical plant facilities. Each board will shape their dashboard report as appropriate to the organization.

Personal Evaluation

Outstanding board leaders are usually known for their decisiveness and fierce resolve. As mentioned earlier, for great Christian leaders, including outstanding board members, you will also find that they—

1. *Speak gracefully.* They watch the words they speak.
2. *Live gratefully.* They don't whine or cry but are grateful.
3. *Listen intently.* They seek first to understand.
4. *Forgive freely.* They are proactive in extending forgiveness.
5. *Lead decisively and humbly.* They harness the power of community life and make decisions with much grace and deep humility.
6. *Care deeply.* They value people, not power.

7. *Pray earnestly.* They believe that God can work in *them* to become the change they desire to see in others.

For more reflection on these core convictions and assumptions, please read "When Good and Godly People Collide over Vision" at <www.BoardServe.org/writing/>. Click the "Writings" tab. Scroll down the list of writings to the paper presented in July 2010 at the Nazarene Seminary of the Americas in San José, Costa Rica.

Appendix 2 and Appendix 3 include a Leader Effectiveness Review. This tool can be used in a variety of ways to regularly evaluate leaders. Additionally, the entire board may choose to answer the statements and discuss the responses as a group. Relate the statements to the core convictions listed above. Encourage your board colleagues to join you in completing the questionnaire.

Summary

Integrity matters. Strong and effective boards *intentionally* engage in mutual accountability, including systematic board development and evaluation.

Packer Thomas Certified Public Accountants & Business Consultants identifies as its company motto "In the long run, only integrity matters. In fact, without integrity, there will be no long run." Affirm integrity as a core value for your board, and find ways to intentionally nurture it "in the long run."

Integrity Matters: Application

Local Church

Integrity has always mattered, and it seems to matter even more in our current culture. One of the essential qualities of leadership on a church board is the quality of *spiritual* leadership. The church is not a secular organization—it is spiritual. The leadership is first and foremost spiritual. Great organizational and leadership minds that are not under the total lordship of Jesus Christ often become a hindrance to the leadership necessary in a local church. Therefore, it is imperative you do all you can to recruit and develop spiritual leaders.

To this end, I developed a leadership response card. This is one of the most effective tools I've ever used. When a person is nominated for leadership on the church board, we let him or her know of the requirements for that role. Before the person agrees to serve in a leadership capacity, he or she is informed of—and must agree to—the qualifications for leadership. We send a leadership response card that must be checked, signed, and returned before the person can be approved for leadership. The card includes these items to check:

☐ I am in right relationship with God.

☐ I am in agreement with the doctrines of the Church of the Nazarene.

☐ I am committed to the mission and vision of the church.

☐ I faithfully tithe at least ten percent of my income through TCC [our local church]

☐ I am currently involved in ministry in the church.
Ministry involved in: _____

_____

☐ I faithfully attend worship at TCC.

☐ I am seeking to be a person of integrity and Christlike character.

☐ I am willing to be part of the team to help accomplish God's purposes for TCC.

☐ If for any reason I find myself in disagreement with any of the above, I will voluntarily resign from the church board.

Not-for-Profit Organization

In contrast to most universities and local churches, not-for-profit organizations are often "stand-alone" units without the benefit of being directly responsible to a denomination or a larger umbrella association. This encumbers the not-for-profit organization with full and direct responsibility to act with integrity.

Organizational integrity—or lack thereof—ultimately determines the impact of the not-for-profit organization. Staff members, persons served, and the broader community expect the organization to operate with integrity. As has been said, "Without integrity nothing else really matters." The effective not-for-profit board comprehends this truth and willingly accepts its responsibility.

To fulfill this responsibility, the effective board does the following:

1. Submits to mutual accountability within the board.
2. Seeks association with another organization to which it will be accountable.
3. Has an annual audit of its finances performed by an independent auditor.
4. Includes policies on board development in its Board Standing Policy Manual (BSPM). Board Source, <www.boardsource. org> noted by LeBron in this chapter, is an excellent source for board development resources.
5. Submits to periodic board and organizational evaluation.
6. Seeks genuine involvement of the entire board in governance and organizational programs and events as appropriate.
7. Systematically evaluates its programs and ministries for effectiveness.

Organizational integrity reflects individual integrity. The Christian not-for-profit board member lives a life of personal integrity and openly pursues deep, authentic spirituality. Gregory Clapper in his book *The Renewal of the Heart Is the Mission of the Church* lists a series of probing "heart" questions (p. 100) helpful for anyone seriously pursuing personal spiritual integrity:

1. Who or what do you now love?

2. In what do you now take joy?

3. What brings you peace?

4. Are you happy now? Why or why not?

5. What makes you afraid?

6. What makes you angry?

7. What makes you impatient?

8. What kinds of actions are you performing in the name of love?

9. How is your life an expression of the joy of your salvation?

10. What kinds of behaviors in your life should be ruled out if you have the peace that passes understanding?

Henry and Richard Blackaby and Claude King in their book *Experiencing God* ask similar questions (p. 85):

1. If you knew that all you had in your life was a relationship with God, would you be totally satisfied?

2. If everything else were removed from you, could you be content having nothing but your relationship with God?

Answering the above questions with humility and honesty will enhance a board member's personal spiritual growth.

Higher Education

The word "intentionally" is prominent in this chapter. Strong and effective boards intentionally plan to strengthen their policies and improve their processes and procedures. These boards intentionally plan for board retreats at least every three years. They are systematic in an evaluation of themselves as board members and their work as boards.

Recently the Africa Nazarene University Board of Trustees (Board of Trust and University Council) convened a two-day planning retreat with an external consultant followed by a full-day meeting as a board to build on what had emerged from the two days of planning.

The goals for the board retreat were as follows:

1. Review strategically the roles and responsibilities of the ANU Board;

2. Affirm board "best practices";
3. Identify goals and action steps necessary for the board to lead the school successfully into the next phase of university life.

The consultant began by discussing the concept that boards evolve and change as the institution grows and matures. If governing boards do not change, the schools soon plateau, and decline is not far behind.

The two-day retreat followed the outline of this book and focused on the best practices of strong and effective boards, and the following twelve best practices were discussed:

1. Board members understand the role, purpose, and function, including the board structure.
2. Board members know, communicate, and make decisions in light of the church's mission, vision, and values.
3. Board members ask the right questions.
4. Board members understand and embrace a board policy manual that contains the board-approved policies for effective and efficient governance of the organization.
5. Board members communicate with each other and address conflict situations as Christians.
6. Board members relate to their leader and the constituency with one voice.
7. Board members intentionally engage in mutual accountability, including systematic board development and evaluation.
8. Board members take time to process decisions and adhere to the practice of "no surprises."
9. Board members embrace change and resolve to work through transitions together and unite for the good of the Kingdom and the advancement of the gospel.
10. Board members participate in assessing the effectiveness of prior decisions and collectively make appropriate adjustments.

11. Board members are outstanding examples of giving regularly and sacrificially to the church, college, or organization they serve.

12. Board members develop new leaders for increased responsibilities and commitment to the organization.

Prior to the discussion of each of these best practices, each board member was asked to identify one word he or she would use to characterize the board. The consultant asked each member to identify one critical issue facing the board. The consultant also wanted to know what one board-related question each member brought to the board retreat. These issues were on the table and referenced throughout the discussion of the characteristics of strong and effective boards.

The latter part of the second day was spent in identifying the board processes to be clarified, policies needed, questions to be asked, plans to be developed, projects to be initiated, and recommendations to the board chairperson for action during the board meeting that follows the two-day retreat.

Eleven "next steps" were identified, and two ad hoc board committees were formed to work on the most crucial of the issues and bring back recommendations for the board to consider in the fall board meeting.

The board is intentional about fulfilling its responsibilities as the university governing board. So can the board on which you serve. Integrity matters!

For more information on the ANU board retreat format, go to <www.BoardServe.org/writings/>. Scroll to "Africa Nazarene University Board Development Workshop Presentation—March 2011."

8

Take Time

Dwight Gunter

Best Practice: Board members take time to process decisions, with no intentional surprises.

The board members and I had become more than acquaintances—we had become friends. I felt it a true privilege and honor to serve as their pastor. Together we could be used by God to make our world different.

After giving myself ample time to evaluate our current situation and to pray for God's leading, I knew there were conversations I had to have with the board regarding vision and direction. There were decisions and changes that were needed if we were going to accomplish the mission as we understood it.

The church board had a desire to construct a new facility for ministry. This dream was living in them even before I arrived as pastor. I saw the dream immediately, and the board and I were together in this. However, economic reality often necessitates a different path to the destination than we perhaps first envisioned. Such was the case, and I now saw a different path to the destination than we all originally saw.

My task wasn't to change the board's mind. Many pastors and other leaders make the mistake of thinking that they alone know the direction the organization should go. They mistakenly believe God has given them stone tablets on their own personal Mt. Sinai and that no one else knows what God is up to. They see it as their job to convince the people to go the way he or she declares to be the will of God. Not so.

Nor was my task to *force* the board to follow what was perhaps indeed the direction of God. Leaders can make the serious mistake of thinking they have the power to force a board into making missional decisions. Although leaders are often vested with certain organizational and structural authority and power, those powers should be exercised with great care and discretion. Some leaders assume they have more authority and power than they actually have.

My task was to explore the new path *with* them to see if it was indeed the will of God for us as a church. It is my firm belief that, as was mentioned earlier, "None of us is as smart as all of us." Part of being an authentic leader is to acknowledge that, as a leader, I don't know everything. There are perspectives I can't see. There are ideas I haven't thought of. There are experiences I haven't lived. There is knowledge I don't possess. There are prayers I haven't prayed and dreams I haven't dreamed.

It is therefore incumbent upon the leader to explore vision and subsequent decisions *with* the board. As leaders, we can then confirm our thoughts and ratify our visions. We can then make more informed and better decisions. None of us is as smart as all of us.

There is also a spiritual assumption underlying this issue: God will speak to whoever will listen. If the board is listening, then God is not going to speak to just one person. He may speak *through* one person, but whoever has ears to hear will indeed hear. The will, vision, and direction of God will become apparent to the leaders.

Here's the rub: this requires time. Leaders and board members need to *take time.*

Time is a hot commodity in today's market. People will spend more money to save more time. We use phrases like "time is valuable" or "don't waste time." People will often pay someone to do what they could do themselves in order to spend their time on a higher priority. People often lament, "If I just had time." Time is precious.

Leaders are often not known for their patience. It seems that for many leaders patience is a learned virtue rather than a natural one.

What we have when we add these two together—the need to take time and the lack of patience—is the recipe for conflict, authoritarianism, or at least bad decisions.

The leader must recognize and intentionally lead within the framework of time.

The board needs time to *process the information* and make a decision. We know from life's experiences that what seems good in a moment may actually be harmful. That which appears to be the right direction on the surface may be devastating in reality. Therefore, living with it for a little while, processing the potential, and pondering the cost of not making a decision all take time. Take a moment to unpack this even more.

The leadership needs to take time to *research the facts*. We live in a world of information, and we have known this for a long time because of all the information that tells us this is so. However, much of the information sold as fact is not necessarily true. Therefore, it becomes incumbent on the leadership to research the facts, thus defining reality. This takes time.

Once the facts are known and reality defined, it is important to take the time to *explore the options*. Often there is more than one route to a destination. What are the options, opportunities, and possibilities available? What is involved in each option? What are the strengths, costs, needs, and benefits of the various options? All these questions take time to explore.

It is also essential for the board to *allow time for the vision to sink in and saturate their thinking*. This involves imagining life as it would be changed by the decision. What would it look like? How would it feel? What would be the secondary benefits of such a decision, direction, or vision? It takes time for the vision to infiltrate the hearts and minds of leaders.

Critical to the decision-making process for the leadership is the necessity to understand the *risks of both action and inaction.* Boards may take the time to process a possibility, but they often overlook the costs associated with indecision and inactivity. What happens if the direction is *not* taken, the decision *not* made, the opportunity *not* seized? Inactivity can be more costly than activity. Doing what has always been done can be riskier than a new direction. It takes time to consider the risks.

Permeating this process is the need to *pray through the issues.* This is crucial if the leadership is seeking God's vision and desiring to join God in His mission in the world. Without the emphasis on prayer, leaders have the tendency to follow their own thinking, their own plans, and their own dreams. Leaders might even be gracious enough to think in terms of a democratic process, thus try to discover the thinking of the majority of leaders.

The kingdom of God is not a democracy. It is a theocracy Therefore, the thoughts and conversations of leadership must be saturated with prayer so the will of God can be known. After all, we pray "your kingdom come, your will be done on earth as it is in heaven." It takes time to pray through the issues.

Once time has been taken to process the information and explore the possibilities, better decisions can be made, the will of God becomes more apparent, and the organization has higher commitment from its constituency. Great boards take time to process decisions.

As a young pastor, I didn't understand this principle. I'm not a patient person by nature, and when I became convinced of the direction the church needed to go, I wanted to be there yesterday. I would get extremely frustrated when the board hesitated to follow my lead.

My wife, Karan, finally got through to me. She helped me see the bigger picture. The truth was, I had lived with the possibilities, researched the facts, processed the change, thought through, prayed through, imagined life after the changes, and grappled with the risks. The board had not. The leadership of the church was busy with their lives, and I thought I was doing them a favor by processing everything *for* them. How foolish I was! How wrong I was!

I had to find a way to take time to process *with* the board. It was essential to bring them into the various phases and steps of visioning and decision-making. This was a major paradigm shift for a twenty-four-year-old impatient pastor. But when I took the time to process it, I realized that my wife was right. My leadership has not been the same since that discovery.

I have had the privilege of pastoring great congregations who took tremendous risks to follow not me but the will and vision of God as we—together—understood it. Looking back, I see that God confirmed it. I cannot help but smile as I think of all God has done because a board *took time* to explore His will. Appendix 10 is an "Action Plan for Local Innovation," designed to lead the process of leader and board learning to walk together in the decision-making process.

Take Time: Application

Local Church

Pastors, journey *with* your people. Lay leaders, journey *with* your pastor. The journey we are on together travels down the road of *time*. Take time.

I am a person who makes decisions quickly. I can give you a plan or a strategy to address a problem without much delay—not that it would be great or even good. Some of our pastoral staff even say my motto is "God loves you, and I have a wonderful plan for your life."

The point I make in this chapter is a real challenge for me personally. Take time.

In my time as pastor I have led our churches in what would be considered as eight different building programs. (I must have been a bad child.) The projects were over $11 million and have consisted of building or remodeling over 145,000 square feet of space. I tell you this to stress the point that taking time does not equate to inactivity. In fact, we take time to ensure that our activity is the will of God.

I've attempted to make it a practice to call the leadership and the entire church to prayer and fasting before making major decisions. When I arrived in Nashville to serve as pastor of TCC, the first thing we did was call the church to forty days of prayer and fasting for the purpose of seeking the vision of God for us as a church. Before we began the first—and second—building projects at TCC, we called for prayer and fasting to precede the church vote. The goal was to seek the will of God.

I believe God speaks. He guides. He directs. He gives leadership—over time.

Therefore, pray until you know—corporately and individually. And when you know, act.

Not-for-Profit Organization

Every person and entity would like to have more of the commodity we call time. Every not-for-profit organizational leader acknowledges the stress that time pressures impose. Leaders constantly search for more volunteers or more funding to increase staff. The needs of not-for-profit organizations always seem to be growing, sometimes exponentially. So the pressure of time always seems to be a primary concern. The effective not-for-profit board knows this is true. When this happens, what should the board do?

The first step is to pause and reflect. As someone has said, "Don't just do something—stand there!" Slow down long enough to provide time for the board and leaders to quietly evaluate the situation. Ask the fundamental questions again:

1. What is our mission? Does this ministry, program, or activity fit within our mission?

2. Are we, the leaders and board, holding each other accountable to our mission? Have we become too busy to dialogue about it?

3. What is our vision? Is what we are doing getting us closer to the vision, or is it cluttering our line of sight to the vision?

4. What are our values? Are we operating within the parameters of our principle values?

5. What is our policy on this? Do we have a policy, or do we need to create one?

6. Are we fulfilling our fiduciary responsibility? Would our donors be pleased with this expenditure of effort?

7. Are we operating within the agreed-upon structure? In the press of time have we deviated from it?

8. Has the board given "permission" to do this—permission in terms of hoping, praying, and expecting effectiveness; giving adequate budgetary and ethical guidelines; not getting too far into the details; providing a climate in which it is safe to fail?

9. Is the board leading or reacting? Is the board leading to a preferred future with a clear, strategic plan, or responding to problems?

After we've examined these issues, the next step is to collectively seek God's guidance. He has promised wisdom; our role is to listen without prejudicing ourselves regarding to whom He may speak.

The effective board knows making the right decisions, especially on strategic issues, requires time for prayer and sufficient deliberation to ensure all perspectives are adequately explored and the knowledge and wisdom of the entire board is brought to bear on the issue. The effective not-for-profit board takes the necessary time to do this. The wise board knows unilateral decisions forced on the board by the leader or by the board on the leader will ultimately be ineffective. This is a journey we are walking together.

Higher Education

Strategic planning for a college, university, or seminary takes time. It is imperative if the institution is to become—or remain—a visionary, vital, and vibrant Holiness institution of higher education. There is no one precise way to proceed in the strategic planning process. The one certainty is that critical thinking and strategic planning are absolutely necessary and should involve the largest number of stakeholders possible. This takes time.

The template used by many school leaders and embraced by the governing boards begins with the *mission* of the college, university, or seminary and clarifies the *raision d'etre* and *purpose* for the existence of the institution. The institutional *vision* focuses on the future and outlines a dream of what the college, university, or seminary can become in the next five to ten years. This template also reaffirms the institutional *values* and ideals inherent in the school's mission and vision.

Guided by these statements and reviewing the results of the SWOT analysis (Strengths, Weaknesses, Opportunities, and Threats), this template identifies the critical initiatives that will need to be addressed strategically, recognizing the systems approach necessary for successful strategic planning and implementation. Each of the strategic initiatives usually includes a paragraph outlining the need for the initiative, followed by the goal statements for the initiative, and, for most goal statements, specific objectives, action steps, time lines, and budget.

Concurrent with the reassessment and strengthening of the mission, vision, values, and guiding principles, it is important to review the history and present status of the school against the backdrop of social, economic, political, and technological forces. Within the context of the institution itself, it is equally important to identify forces that would have positive or negative impacts on the school's ability to accomplish the mission and realize the vision over the next five to ten years. The results of this collaborative analysis, review, revisions, and focused discussions bring forth initiatives that focus on any or all of the following:

Academic programs, on and off campus

Campus facilities

Technology

A secure financial base for campus operations and programs

The quality of student life

Campus-wide ministry and mission

Spiritual renewal, leadership training, and ministry development

Faculty and staff development

Institutional collaboration

Recruitment and retention of students

Ensuring financial viability.

Again, each critical initiative you select and include in the strategic plan should include a brief rationale, a statement of goals, and supportive specific objectives, action steps, time lines, and budget.

Some individuals will lament that the strategic planning process takes too much time and is too aggressive; others will complain that the process goes too fast and does not go far enough. You just need to begin. It will take time, because you will involve a large number of people. The board needs to drive the process.

Because what emerges is a *strategic* plan, it will be revised regularly to assure that changing contingencies are being addressed as the board, administration, faculty, and staff, as well as other stakeholders, work together toward accomplishing the mission and realizing the vision and shared dream for the institution you love and serve.

9

Yes! to Missional Change

Dwight Gunter

Best Practice: Board members embrace change and resolve to work through transitions together and unite for the good of the Kingdom and the advancement of God's mission.

Recently our eighteen-month-old grandson walked to his diaper bag, selected a diaper, and brought it to his GiGi—along with the wipes! I thought, *That boy likes change—but chances are that he'll grow out of it.* Most people do.

"Change" is often viewed as a long four-letter word. It doesn't sit well on the palate. Churches have struggled with changes occurring over the last fifty years. It seems as if the rate and scope of change have been injected with steroids and have accelerated beyond comprehension.

How can leaders address this issue?

Change is not limited to a church or to a nonprofit organization. Change is everywhere and on all levels.

For example, how we express our faith is changing. Look at the changes in church attendance, church commitment, community-building, ethnicity, and worship styles. The list is endless.

The changes in our faith expressions are consistent with the changes in our culture: economy, ethnic demographics, educational expectations and opportunities, life expectancy, technology, family, spiritual pursuits. Again, the list is endless.

How can leaders address this issue?

Far too many churches have vehemently resisted it. Some churches have been paralyzed by fear and an anti-change reaction and therefore refuse to make the needed changes. People cling desperately to the past, to what is familiar, to their infamous comfort zone. Change always involves the loss of something, and as someone remarked, "No organization is so out of order that somebody doesn't like it as it is."

Change seems to be tolerable if it is directed toward others, but not acceptable if we ourselves are affected. Think about the changes you've experienced in recent years. What changes have you encountered in the past eighteen months? What changes are you facing in the next year? Is change good? Sometimes. Is change inevitable? Always!

Obviously some people are going to be resistant to change. *That's an intentional understatement, by the way.*

My mother and I were talking about change a few years ago and asked the common question of how many Christians it takes to change a light bulb. You know the obvious answer: seven. One to change the bulb and six to resist the change. However, do you know the conversation that preceded the decision?

First person: Wasn't that a wonderful old light bulb? Why, I remember stories about putting that light bulb in place. I grew up on that light bulb.

Second person: My grandmother bought that light bulb, and my grandfather put it in.

Third person: You don't have the authority to change that light bulb. You can't do that. It's not in the manual or bylaws. If you do it, I'll write the authorities. I'll contact your superiors.

Fourth person: I'll write the anonymous letter to the pastor, slandering his [her] character and attacking his [her] family because he [she] suggested that someone might want to change the light bulb that no longer works.

Fifth person: Why don't we build a showcase so we'll never forget the old light bulb?

Sixth person: If we're going to build a showcase, we first need to appoint a committee to build it.

By the time they finished their discussion, another light bulb needs to be changed. And the pastor says, "Why don't we just stay in the dark?"

That's the problem with churches that resist change as if such resistance is a spiritual gift. They live in the dark rather than walk in the light.

It is somewhat understandable, however, when considering what change really means. There are reasons people resist change.

- All change represents a *loss* of something.
- Change often challenges a person's sense of *control.*
- Some people resist change in order to *get even* with the organization because of prior changes they didn't like.
- Some resist because they feel the organization is about to make a *mistake,* and they care deeply about the organization.

However, resisting change can do more harm than good. Resisting change takes effort, and there are more productive ways to spend energy. Resisting change can be extremely divisive in a church, and in such cases no one wins. Instead of resisting change, people need to grasp the future.

George Barna states that churches too often make the mistake of refusing to change or waiting until it is too late to make the necessary change. "One of the most important lessons the American church must absorb is that patience may be harmful to the church's health" (Barna, *Second Coming*, p. 43).

How can leaders address this issue?

It is helpful in addressing the issue of change to understand the stages of change. There are multiple theories about the stages of change, but there are some common elements to the theories.

First is an *acknowledgement* of a need or of a failing system. Sometimes this occurs because of pain or hurt. Sometimes it occurs because of the possibility of some type of reward. Sometimes it occurs because other changes force it, and there is simply no choice. We must acknowledge it. Raymond Hurn once stated to me, "In a failing system, more of the same is not the answer."

Second, this acknowledgement of need is followed by *research*. Information regarding the need is necessary. What are others doing to address this? What approaches have been tried and resulted in success—or were unsuccessful? What are all the facts involved? What are the ramifications of various decisions? What are the results of not addressing the need? The answers to these questions will begin to form a solution to the need.

The third stage is the *decision*. Deciding the course of action is seldom easy. Not every need has an easy fix. Sometimes the necessary change is simply less problematic than other solutions. People can be critical of leadership because the change is not flawless. The fact is this: changes are rarely flawless; therefore, expectations need to be realistic.

Unforeseen pain is often experienced when dealing with change. This fourth stage can be very frustrating. Doing the right things sometimes produce the wrong results. The temptation will be to quit, give up, or revert. You may need to make some adjustments in order to continue, but those adjustments are worth it. Keep going.

After a while the fifth stage of change occurs: *assimilation*. The changes are assimilated into the life of the organization and become the new normal.

This process from acknowledgement of a need to assimilation of a change can be gruesome and taxing. Yet we cannot live without change. Change is inevitable!

Again I ask, *How can leaders address this issue?* Is there a way for leaders to embrace change and resolve to work through transitions together, united for the good of the Kingdom and the advancement of God's mission? The answer is yes—a certain, assured *yes.* Leaders who effectively lead through change accept and encourage others to do the following:

1. **Be open to change.** One significant leadership principle is—you can work only with people who are willing to work with you. The leadership must be open to change if needs are going to be addressed and failing systems are going to be made effective.

2. **Encourage participation by those most affected by the changes.** Plan solutions and creative ideas *with* others. Educate people most affected by the possible changes.

3. **Choose your battles wisely.** Uncle Buddy Robinson is credited with saying, "A bulldog can whip a skunk; but it just ain't worth it."

4. **Test every proposed change for compatibility with Scripture, theology, the mission, and the values of the organization.** Not every idea is consistent with these, and yet compatibility is a necessity for the organization to have integrity.

5. **Lead from a pastoral perspective.** The leadership needs to know and love the congregation. There needs to be appreciation and empathy for where people are in their spiritual development, the stage of life they are in, and their experiences.

6. **Give people time and space to assimilate change.** Leadership will often struggle with change proposals, taking time to work through issues and solutions. Grant this same opportunity to others who have not been part of the process. Don't make the mistake of expecting others to be supportive from

the moment the changes are presented. Give time and space for processing the changes.

7. **Connect the changes to the mission.** Change for the sake of change is not necessarily a good thing. Missional change is. All change should be connected to the mission in order that the mission can be accomplished and resources are not wasted.

8. **Seek the presence of the Holy Spirit.** God is active among us. If the leadership has prayed and sought the will of God, then expect the Holy Spirit to be at work in the church.

9. **Remember that God is Lord, and we are not.** It is imperative for leadership to remember that this is about the advancement of God's kingdom, not the leadership's kingdom. That means God has a vested interest in the effectiveness of His Church, His people, His kingdom.

10. **Invent the future instead of redesigning the past.** This is crucial. "The best way to predict the future is to invent it. . . . Be purposeful. Look at what's needed now, and set about doing it" (Price Pritchett and Ron Pound, *The Employee Handbook for Organizational Change*, p. 40). We need people whose vision of the future is stronger than their memory of the past. We need churches whose desire for the future advancement of the kingdom of Christ is greater than their love of the past—or even of the present. We need leaders who will embrace missional change.

It is imperative for leadership to *model* for our culture how to initiate meaningful change and how to respond to change. The Church should never propagate the myth that God is against change. The emotional resistance to change is often a poor reflection on God. The refusal to find creative ways to enact missional change is inconsistent with the ways of God.

A synonym for change is *innovation*. An important guiding force for innovation is an understanding of the heart of God. God is an innovator; God is a change agent; God is a catalyst for transformation; God is all about innovation and change.

Jesus was an innovator. He even offered a "new covenant."

The innovative Holy Spirit brought about a new approach in the life of God's people. Gentiles were grafted into the Church. This was a major change that some never accepted. Ask the apostle Paul.

"Innovation . . . must spring from a love affair with what God loves" (Rob Wilkins, *Life@Work,* March/April 1999, vol. 2, no. 2, p. 44). Christians and the Church must love what God loves so much that they are willing to be creative in serving. It is the heart of God that should cause the Church to be change agents.

Could it be that in order to be true to our heritage as the people of God, a local church needs to be innovative? Change and innovation are at the heart of the mission of God. Change should be a constant in the life of the Church. God makes changes. Thanks be to God!

So, Ben, our grandson, walks over to GiGi and hands her a diaper. He may grow out of wanting change, but he'll never grow out of facing it.

Yes! to Missional Change: Application

Local Church

Change happens. Sometimes we look back and wonder just how it all changed. Sometimes we look ahead and pray for it all to change. Nevertheless, change happens.

How do we create missional change?

Having to deal with so much change prompted me to create a process for it. Most people oppose the way change occurs as much—if not more—than the change itself. I've outlined the process below, but for more detailed information, see Appendix 10.

Phase One. Informational constituency presentation: congregation, church board, or the organization responsible for leading the change

The purpose of Phase One is to inform the constituency of the proposed change. It is also to begin the process of gathering feedback from the constituency.

Phase Two. Response presentation to the leadership: team making the decision

The purpose of this phase is to present to the leadership the responses gathered in Phase One.

Phase Three. Second constituency presentation

The purpose of this phase is to report to the constituency the results of the first two phases and the current status of the change. More feedback can be collected if desired.

Phase Four. Straw poll/survey

The purpose of this phase is to quantify the issue. Leadership needs to know what the people are sensing concerning the will of God.

Phase Five. Final decision by the leadership team: Pass or defeat.

The purpose of this phase is simply to make a decision.

Phase Six. Assure the people that the change will be reevaluated after a sufficient time period for success.

The purpose of this phase is to let the people know that effectiveness is the goal.

This is simply *a* plan for navigating change. It is not the only one, but it has worked well for me.

Not-for-Profit Organization

In the not-for-profit world, change is systemic. Much of the world that not-for-profits serve is in a constant state of flux. The needs of humanity change, formal sources of financial support change, informal sources of support change, volunteer support changes, communication methods change, local, state, and federal regulations change, and on it goes. Change is inevitable.

For not-for-profit organizations, many of these changes are imposed from the outside. The first questions are "Are we at the mercy of change imposed on us?" "Are we doomed to live a reactionary life?" "Should we hunker down into a protective bunker?" The answer is absolutely not! We must not accept a victim mind-set. The next questions, which follow close behind, are "How do we handle change imposed on us?" "What can we do?"

1. To begin with, the effective not-for-profit board knows that the more thorough the planning, the less devastating the inevitable changes. As a policy of the board standing policy manual, the board asks the executive director to work with the staff to develop two plans. The first is a one-year *working plan* that clarifies the goals, issues, challenges, and major outcomes established for the current year. The second is a *strategic plan* that sets the direction for the next three to five years. Those plans, after board input and approval, become the working documents that guide the organization's effort and activity.

2. Develop early-warning mechanisms to seek out potential changes coming from the outside as early as possible. Build bridges to the organization's various constituencies. Engage decision-makers in conversation. Ask questions of leaders such as "What is happening in local, state, and federal govern-

ment that may affect us?" "Is the community leadership changing?" "Is the local community's sentiment about us strong and improving?" "Is this major donor's stage of life changing?"

3. Evaluate data available from inside the organization. Ask ministry-related questions such as "Are we seeing more poverty-related needs?" "Is domestic violence increasing?" Ask fund-related questions such as "Is the average donation increasing or decreasing?" Is the number of donors increasing or decreasing?"

4. Build all changes, whether from outside or inside, into the *working plan* and *strategic plan*.

5. Develop a strong competency of adjusting to changing ministry situations and creating new ministries.

6. Employ the ten steps listed in this chapter as a pattern for embracing change and working through transitions.

7. Whether the change is imposed from outside, by an intentional decision of the organization, or is a surprise, the effective not-for-profit board helps the persons involved work through the five stages of change noted in this chapter.

Higher Education

Change management in higher education draws the inspiration of the Sigmoid—or S—curve, which reflects the life cycle of an organization, especially the dynamics and challenges of new beginnings. The energy required to start a new organization changes as it comes into contact with the forces of day-to-day existence, development, and growth.

The leadership strengths that brought a higher education institution, local congregation, or mission agency into existence and nurtured it to take root and grow can, if not adapted, become the source of institutional plateauing and decline. Organizations evolve and change; so must their governing boards. Transitions occur and must be managed successfully in order for organizational growth to continue.

The image below illustrates briefly the reality that leadership must strategically move ahead of the curve to transform the organization before a downward turn. The beauty in the modified S-curve illustration is in the hope it displays. There is hope for the organization you lead, no matter where it finds itself along the life cycle of the S-curve. Governing boards of colleges, universities, and seminaries may choose to involve consultants in board development to assist them in managing the transitions required for continued growth in organizational life.

For more information on the Sigmoid curve, read Marty Baker's explanation at <http://creativitycentral.squarespace.com/creativity -central/2010/3/8/creativity-and-the-sigmoid-curve.html>

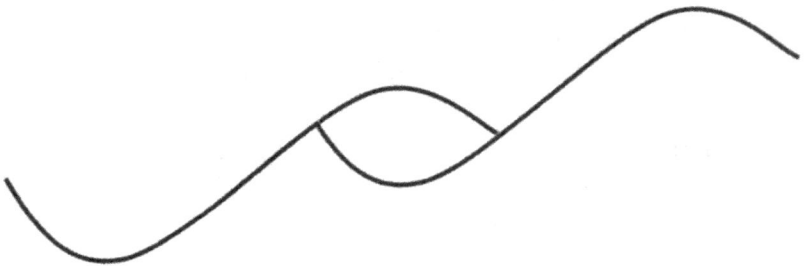

Look closely at the modified S curve.

Understanding transitions is important for the leader. The Sigmoid curve helps us conceptualize inevitable transition in the higher education institutions, local churches, or ministry organizations you serve. Questions for school—and other—leaders:

Do higher education institutions go through numerical—and spiritual—cycles?

Are the cycles inevitable?

How do they regain momentum in the midst of cycles?

In the book *Managing Transitions: Making the Most of Change*, by William Bridges, organized cycles are discussed in the context of change and transitions. This foundational understanding of organizational cycles enlightens a perspective of the S curve.

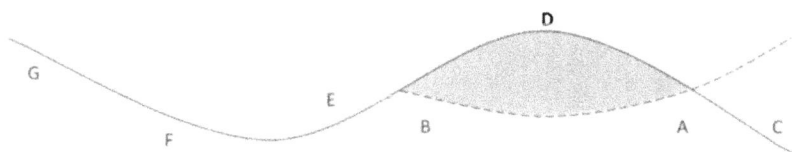

A. Point of initiative: someone has a dream

B. Time of resourcing the Vision: you slow down to resource your dream

C. Growth: the vision takes hold

D. When the organization is most effective and efficient

E. Decline: when the same things are done as in earlier years

F. Breakout time/vision: takes place during "prime" time

G. Turnaround vision: a crucial point when leadership has responsibility to start a new "S" curve

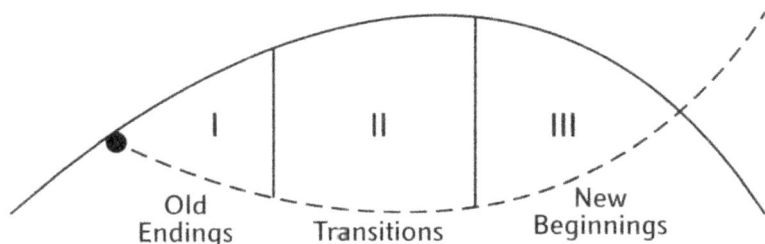

A breakout view of F through G section above:

The leader must ask, "What are the old endings that must go?" "What are the core values of the old that must be retained?"

Regarding the *transition* period, the leader's role is to articulate the end vision but retain core convictions. The leader during this period of change and transition must model consistency, steadiness, integrity, respect, trust, and communication.

Regarding new beginnings, the leader and board must engage the stakeholders in institutionalizing the transition through which you are going and toward which you are moving. The leader must continue to model the Christian character qualities of Ephesians 4 and 1 Peter 1, especially in conflict situations and with constituents who differ with you.

There is a critical time when the school administration and board have the responsibility to start a new S curve. Further questions for leader and board:

1. Where is your school in the cycle?
2. What should be the role of board and school leadership in this cycle?
3. What should be the role of college, university or seminary president regarding "F" and "G" transition points?

Managing the transitions can either facilitate or derail the change we envision and need in the organization we serve.

10
Review/Revise/
Redirect/
Renew
Dwight Gunter

Best Practice: Board members participate in
assessing the effectiveness of prior decisions and
collectively make appropriate adjustments.

I grew up watching the television series *Star Trek,* the original, real
one, not the no-longer-new series. Okay, so I'm dating myself. But
most people know the opening lines of the series, thanks to the re-
runs and the subsequent movies: "Space, the final frontier. These are
the voyages of the starship *Enterprise.* Its five-year mission: to explore strange new worlds, to seek out new life and new civilizations,
to boldly go where no man has gone before." Can't you just hear the
60s theme song in the background?

Look at this opening monologue by Captain James T. Kirk. It contains the foundations for assessing the effectiveness of the organization.

First, the context is given: "Space, the final frontier."

Next comes the organization itself: "the starship *Enterprise.*"

Finally comes the mission, complete with time frame for measuring results: "to explore . . . to seek . . . to go."

Maybe this metaphor is a stretch, but I don't think so. Boards have a natural tendency to forget the context and the mission while becoming overly focused on the daily operations of survival. In the process they tend to lose their sense of identity.

Once the context, sense of identity, and mission are lost, assessing the progress of the organization is pointless. That would be akin to checking how far you have to travel to get to nowhere in particular. Therefore, there are three essential elements that must be in place if an organization is to assess the effectiveness of prior decisions.

First, it is necessary for previous decisions to be based on an accurate understanding of the *context* in which the organization exists. In the case of Trevecca Community Church, which I pastor, the factors that define our context are as follows:

- A university campus
- Inner city
- Senior adult housing
- Many suburban members
- Denominational loyalty and traditions
- Creative/Progressive mentality

The *context* must be identified along with the needs, challenges, resources, and benefits associated with each component. Imagine creating a story. The context is the setting in which the story unfolds. Understanding the story—grasping the meaning of the story—is based on knowing that context.

The second essential element is a sense of *identity*. Who is the organization? What are the defining traits? What are its core values? Our identity at Trevecca Community Church is defined as a Christian church in general and a Church of the Nazarene in particular. Go back to the creation of the story. Every story has characters. They are the action figures of the narrative. As the story unfolds, the characters are identified, defined, and developed.

A third essential element is a well-defined *mission*. The organization must not only know its mission, but also the mission must be internalized. It must be part of the DNA of the organization. It is assumed that previous decisions are based on that well-defined mission. In the case of Trevecca Community Church, the mission involves discipleship, worship, evangelism, relationship-building, and compassionate ministries: all flowing to and through the context. Look again at the story concept. Every story has a setting, characters, a problem, and solutions. The identification of the problem along with the potential solutions forms the plot. In other words, the mission is the plot.

With these elements in place, the organization can now assess prior decisions. But another question arises: What does it actually mean to *assess* or to *conduct an assessment*? Fundamentally, assessment has to do with measuring desired outcomes. Simply stated, when assessing prior decisions, the leadership should ask if the prior decisions were directed toward the context, reflective of who the organization is, and consistent with the stated mission.

Assessments are designed to identify the current reality. Where does the organization stand currently? What is the situation? What is the story at present? What progress is being made? Has the objective been accomplished or not?

Assessment is a process. It should be an ongoing process occurring at least annually if not semi-annually.

Assessments ask questions in light of context, identity, and mission in regards to effectiveness. What's working? What needs improvement? What needs to be eliminated? What needs to be changed? What needs to be repeated? Identify the priorities—two to four are enough—and next steps to accomplishing the objectives.

Assessments can be directed to virtually anything and everything.

- Finances
- Programs
- Events
- Ministries
- Personnel

- Leadership development
- Customer satisfaction

Assessments are based on good objectives. When the objectives are clear, they can be assessed.

Assessments reflect intentionality. When an organization conducts regular assessments, it is communicating the fact that it is intentional about accomplishing the mission. Assessments make a statement that the mission matters. Assessments express the seriousness and the importance of the mission.

Basically, an assessment attempts to determine if the mission is being accomplished. Is the organization doing what it intends to do? Is it being what it claims to be? Is it focused where it should be focused?

The benefits of conducting assessments can be tremendous. Through the process of assessing the effectiveness of outcomes and goals, desired results eventually can be achieved and sustained. The effectiveness of organizations is naturally inclined to be short-lived. Leaders can hold too tightly to what has worked in the past in spite of failing effectiveness in the present. It is easy to forget the principle that "what got you to the present might not get you to the desired future." One of the benefits of continual assessments is that it leads to sustaining desired results.

By conducting ongoing assessments, the leadership can modify, discard, or create new goals. This offers the potential for the organization to be even more effective in accomplishing its mission within its context. Effectiveness is the goal.

Another benefit regards resources. In not-for-profit organizations particularly, resources are often scarce and must be tightly managed. No one desires to be wasteful, but particularly nonprofits. Assessing the effectiveness of the organization can reduce the wasting of resources. Who wants to fund ministries that are no longer effective? Who wants to invest time in programs that are not successful? Assessments allow an organization to maximize its resources, putting them into the people and systems that are closest to the heart of the mission.

Also, conducting assessments can lead to a sense of meaning. The members of the organization realize that they, along with their work, are valuable and meaningful. When people know their work makes a difference, they work with a greater sense of intentionality.

So how does an organization conduct assessments? It is beyond the scope of this chapter—and even this book—to discuss all the ways in which assessments can be conducted. There is no shortage of materials on conducting assessments. There are needs assessments, personnel assessments, program assessments, and systems assessments. They can be found anywhere from bookstores to the Internet. Here is a general overview.

Step One: Review

The leadership of the organization should begin an assessment with a review of the context, the identity of the organization, and identification of the mission. The purpose of the review is to make sure all the leaders are on the same page as they travel to the same destination.

Step Two: Revise

Sometimes, in fact quite often, organizations are exploring new territory. Like the starship *Enterprise,* an organization may not have passed through a particular solar system before. Organizations often try to solve problems and accomplish mission in creative ways, not having travelled that way before. By assessing what is effective or ineffective, the various components of the organization can be revised. Goals can be changed, modified, or eliminated. Personnel can be redirected or added. Systems can become more efficient.

Step Three: Redirect

Redirect personnel, resources, and energy to better accomplish the revised mission, vision, goals, and objectives. There may be some approaches that are not necessarily broken but are unnecessary; that is, the purpose it was to fulfil is already being accomplished in other ways. Therefore, resources directed to those areas can and should be redirected to areas that are in need.

Step Four: Renew

The leadership of the organization needs to renew their commitment to the mission. They need to lead all the members of the organization in a renewal of commitment. Sometimes people grow tired and lose focus. An assessment should provide renewed energy and motivation for the mission ahead.

Context is crucial. Understanding our identity is vitally important. Mission matters. Even with these in place, without assessing the effectiveness of the organization, the desired results would be achieved haphazardly or coincidentally at best.

Great boards assess effectiveness. They review, revise, redirect, and renew.

Beam me up, Scottie. Let's get going.

Review/Revise/Redirect/Renew: Application

Local Church

Five basic questions surface as we think about this issue.

What is our context? Is it inner city? Suburbs? Rural?

Demographic data will prove very helpful in answering these questions and determining the context of a local church. Usually denominations have access to demographic data, and in many cases it is free of charge.

Who are we? It would be revealing for the leadership of a local church to describe and identify *who* their church is. An exercise for the leadership could be to role-play this conversation. Imagine having to describe your church to someone who knows nothing about its denominational affiliation, history, theology, mission, personality, people, and so on. How would you describe it to them? This exercise could help your leadership identify and own its identity.

What is our mission? This issue has been sufficiently presented in earlier chapters in various ways. Work toward memorizing the mission, and keep it visually in front of the leadership.

How are we doing? This deals with review/assessment.

The first step in the assessment is to simply ask, *Did we do what we said we were going to do? Did we actually do the ministries we said we were going to do?*

The second step is to ask the effectiveness questions. Are we impacting our context as we said we were going to do in our mission statement? Are we reaching who we said we were going to reach? How can we do it more effectively?

What resources do we need to redirect in order to accomplish our mission? This will involve human, financial, and even facilities resources. Churches often find that they are doing too much in one area and not enough in another. Sometimes churches have to eliminate some things that are working but are overkill in a particular ministry focus in order to have the resources available for an area that is under-targeted or neglected altogether.

Not-for-Profit Organization

Not-for-profit organizations seem to be especially susceptible to the changing direction of "today's ministry" winds. A specific cause catches the interest of the media or a community leader, and it becomes popular to meet that need; then soon another cause receives attention, and the temptation is to meet that need. Changing with the winds, succumbing to mission drift, or giving in to a financially opportunistic bent can be devastating to the organization's mission.

To avoid this, the first step is for the not-for-profit board to build the principle of assessment into the organization's DNA. The board standing policies manual is the appropriate place to acknowledge the importance of assessment and create a process to periodically evaluate prior decisions and actions. The board should take the lead and periodically assess its own work. Doing this legitimizes the process, thereby giving "permission" to every component of the organization to assess its work. Of course, assessment assumes that desired outcome or goals, objectives, and accomplishments have been established. If not, now is the time to set them.

In this chapter Dwight talks about the importance of clarifying the organization's context, identity, and mission. Another Christian consulting group refers to an organization's code, context, and calling. Both are asking the same questions: Who are we? What are the characteristics of the setting in which God has placed us? What are we supposed to do about it? Answering these three questions provides the basis for initially setting desirable outcomes.

They also provide the basis for assessing our progress. All three have the possibility of change. Major changes in paid or volunteer staff, planned or unplanned, may change who we are. The community or neighborhood in which we serve may be gradually or suddenly hosting new ethnic groups, or a major employer may move, which changes our context. Any of these changes may change what we are supposed to do. Even if who we are and where we minister do not change, what we are supposed to do may still change.

All these possibilities beg for regular reevaluation and assessment in the not-for-profit organization.

One excellent process a not-for-profit organization can use for self-assessment is the four-step process presented in this chapter.

Review: *Has our context changed?* Is the economy in our ministry area thriving or declining? Has the demographic description changed?

Have we changed? Are we the same organization? Are we more dependent on grant funding? Has leadership changed the direction of the organization?

Have our outcomes changed? Did we do the ministries we said we would do? Are our ministries as effective as we planned? Are we reaching the right population?

Revise: On the basis of the review, what decisions do we need to revisit? What adjustments of goals, personnel, or systems are needed?

Redirect: Based on the review, what areas need more or fewer resources?

Renew: Is everyone still on board with the organization? Should we renew our personal commitment?

Another excellent tool to evaluate organizational capacity and prioritize development is the APEX Project's Legal and Program Audit, which is described below in the Higher Education Application of this chapter.

A third method of assessment is to secure the expertise of a trained consultant to lead the process.

Whatever assessment method is used, the process is as important as the initial development of mission, vision, and values, because the not-for-profit world changes.

Higher Education

Reading this chapter reminded me again of the imperative to continually review and revise your planning strategy in the ministry assignment in which God has placed you. Early in my leadership responsibilities I feared the words "review and revise," because I thought they would suggest to the board that I had not thought through all the challenges and planned accordingly. How foolish of me!

Soon I began to realize that I could become paralyzed in the process of decision-making if I waited until I had all the answers before a strategic idea was shared with the board regarding the future of the organization. Placing the review and revision component in the center of the planning process enabled me to give my best regarding thoughts for the future or a significant program idea, acknowledging that my "best" would be revised—for the better!

With a draft on the table, the process was accelerated, because the board had a plan to be considered. Embracing the revisions freed me as the school leader to utilize the board—or board executive committee—as a sounding board for ideas and plans I was considering. What I did not realize was that the very process was empowering for the board. They felt part of the planning process and more easily embraced the decision when decision-making was required!

The following planning model illustrates this process of planning, which naturally includes continual review and revision throughout the process.

Planning Model

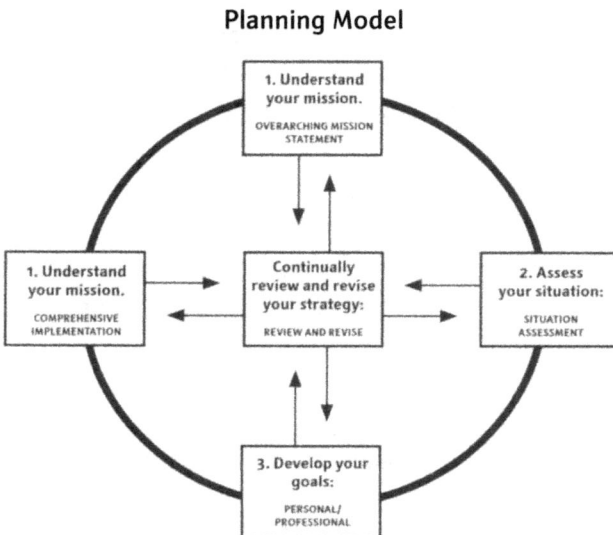

Another tool for the assessment of the higher education institution is the Legal and Program Audit, developed by Nazarene Compassionate Ministries Inc. (NCMI).

The APEX Project is an assessment tool developed by NCMI to assist faith-based organizations and non-government organizations (FBOs/NGOs) in identifying "areas of organizational capacity and areas that need development." The audit can be modified for use by colleges, universities, and seminary boards in an assessment and audit of the legal and program areas of the school on whose board they serve and govern.

On the basis of the information gained from the audit, the boards and school administration can prioritize and address those areas in need of correction, improvement, and support.

The APEX Project enables school leaders, organization directors, church pastors, and board chairpersons to conduct legal and program audits on the schools, companies, or churches they lead. Categories include the following:

- Legal documentation checklist
- Mission/vision/values/strategic planning
- Board development
- Financial accountability
- Fund development
- Human resources
- Program development
- Organizational capacity
- Priorities for capacity building

For instance, for the category of "Legal documentation," on a scale of 1 to 4, the leader identifies the organization's level of compliance in areas such as—

- Articles of incorporation
- Bylaws
- 501(c3) status
- Payroll documentation
- IRS 990 form

- Insurance
- Legal/financial advisors
- Registered agent and current contact address

For sure, not every item identified in the "legal documentation" category will apply equally toward all schools and/or nonprofit organizations. Some states may require additional information from the organization. However, the APEX Project is an excellent start on a legal and program audit.

To read more about the NCMI Organizational Development Assessment tool, or to view the full APEX Project online, please go to <http://www.nazarenecompassion.org/CMCs/APEXAssessment/tabid/534/Default.aspx>.

11
Role Models of Generosity and Stewardship
LeBron Fairbanks

Best Practice: Board members are outstanding examples of giving regularly and sacrificially to the church, college, or organization they serve.

One of the most memorable and profoundly moving experiences in ministry was my involvement in the Lausanne 2004 Conference on World Evangelism in Pattaya, Thailand. Participants were asked to join one of thirty "issue groups," with each group assigned to a critical issue facing the Church and its mission in the new century. Prior to the conference I was asked to co-lead issue group #27, "Funding for Evangelism and Mission." My colleague in leading the group was MacMillian Kiiru, from Nairobi, Kenya.

Charles Roost and I served as co-editors of the article reflecting the work of the group for a Lausanne book summarizing the work of the conference. The majority of the twenty-seven ministry leaders in our group represented several types of ministries and led ministries in various countries in what is commonly called "the developing world." Together we addressed the funding subject given to us.

It was in those Thailand meetings that the word "generosity" came to mean much more than the "bigness" of money given. Rather, from a biblical perspective it refers to a quality of spirit and attitude reflected in both givers and receivers. Both donors and recipients must guard their attitudes and spirits as they serve as role models of generosity and stewardship. Board members of colleges, local churches, and ministry organizations not only set examples of faithful and consistent giving to the organizations on whose boards they serve, but they also reflect a quality of spirit and attitude of respect and gratitude toward the givers, donors, or tithers who sacrificially give small or large amounts of money to the Christian ministry. Another best practice of strong and effective boards is that they also serve as role models of generosity and stewardship.

Let's Review

Earlier in the book we discussed the necessity of board members to focus on the mission, vision, and values of the organization, institution, or local church they serve. A mission statement is about the basic purposes of the organization. It is a statement about the organization's reasons for existing.

Remember the theme of chapter three? The section focused on the importance of asking the right questions. Mission statements often grow out of discussions around questions referenced in the earlier chapter:

- Who are we?
- Where are we?
- Where are we going?
- How will we get there?
- Why is it important to get there?
- What makes us distinctive or unique?

The mission statement clarifies an organization's primary intentions. An organization is a means to an end. It is not an end in itself. The organization serves a greater purpose than the organization itself. A mission statement will define the organization's role, bring focus to activity, and eliminate ambiguity concerning its reason for being.

Vision, on the other hand, is a "hear" and "see" word. It suggests a future orientation, an image of what the organization might look like in, say, ten years. It suggests an end result and connotes a standard of excellence. A vision statement is a mental image of a possible and desirable future state of the organization.

Values tell us how we expect to travel to where we want to go. It describes how we intend to operate as we pursue our vision. Governing values would include an understanding of the lines we will not cross, how we expect to regard the donors, tithers, the students, the campus community, the congregation, and how we want to behave toward one another.

The Challenge

God often chooses to use the resources of this world to accomplish His work. Human resources and financial resources seem to be those most significant in the work of the Church. History proves that funding for evangelism and mission is very important for the work of the Kingdom.

The funding of evangelism and mission has hosted both great achievements for the benefit of the Kingdom and significant pain and economic abuse within the Body of Christ. As was demonstrated in Christ's ministry and the life of the Early Church, money is a God-given tool for catalyzing mission, but when used without integrity and good stewardship, it has the potential to create significant harm.

The challenges faced in the funding arena seem to fall into three categories:

1. Shortage of funds to accomplish reasonable goals.

2. Misuse of funds on the part of ministry personnel and organizations.

3. Distortion of biblical principles and standards in fund development.

The Current Scene in Mission Funding

The current environment in funding mission and vision is generally characterized by a vertical, top/down arrangement in which the money from donors trickles down to the recipient organization or ministry.

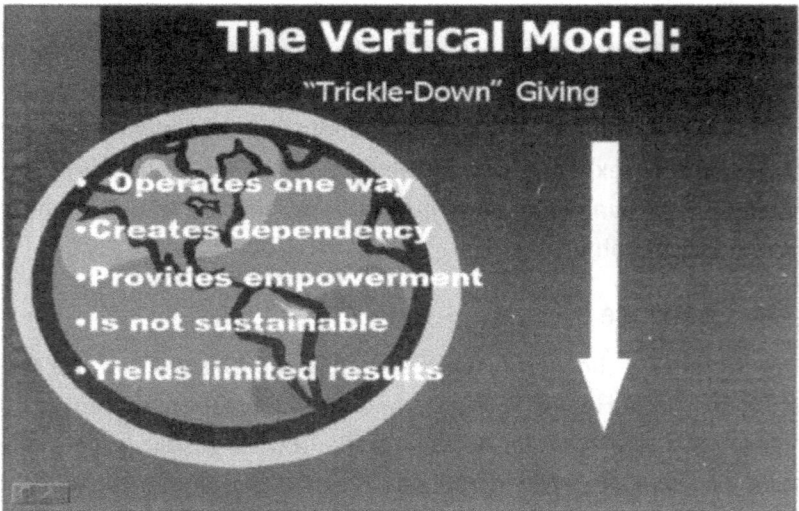

The Vertical Model:
"Trickle-Down" Giving

• Operates one way
• Creates dependency
• Provides empowerment
• Is not sustainable
• Yields limited results

This vertical model, because of its hierarchical nature, has created major problems within the Body of Christ. The donor has been reduced to a "source" for funds. The ministry organization has been reduced to "operators" of fundraising schemes primarily related to organizational budgets. Missing in the model is the character that honors biblical principles for the effective use of God's resources to accomplish His purposes. The top/down relationship within the Body of Christ disfigures stewardship and cries out for redemption and transformation.

A New Model

What is required is acceptance of the proper theology of funding and subsequent practices that will point the Church to fulfillment of the task of mission and vision while affirming the equality of all believers and unity within the Body of Christ.

The challenges in funding evangelism in the current environment can be traced back to the lack of an adequate theological framework for the role stewards play as they manage financial resources. In the absence of a comprehensive theology and a reflecting set of principles for financial resources, the world of nonprofits has fallen prey to ineffective models and strategies characterized by the following:

- Lack of a functional theology regarding fund development and resource management.
- Lack of mutual understanding, effective strategies, and clear funding models concerning the biblical relationship between giver and receiver.
- An assumption of limited local resources available to the emerging church and the lack of effective leadership in the management of resources.
- Education and training that are sufficient in stewardship and fund development at both ministry leadership training institutions and local congregations for funders in mission strategy for mission agency executives and their development staffs.
- Attitudes of dependence on the part of receivers and co-dependence on the part of providers. The new model, strongly recommended by Lausanne Issue Group #27, "Funding Evangelism and Mission," changes the way giving and receiving are perceived, approached, and accomplished. It is recommended with the understanding that such a major paradigm shift will not be easily adopted.

This model, called the "Mutual Commitment" model, is horizontal in structure, placing all parties in the fund development effort on an equal plane. In this model all believers enjoy an equal standing before the throne of Christ.

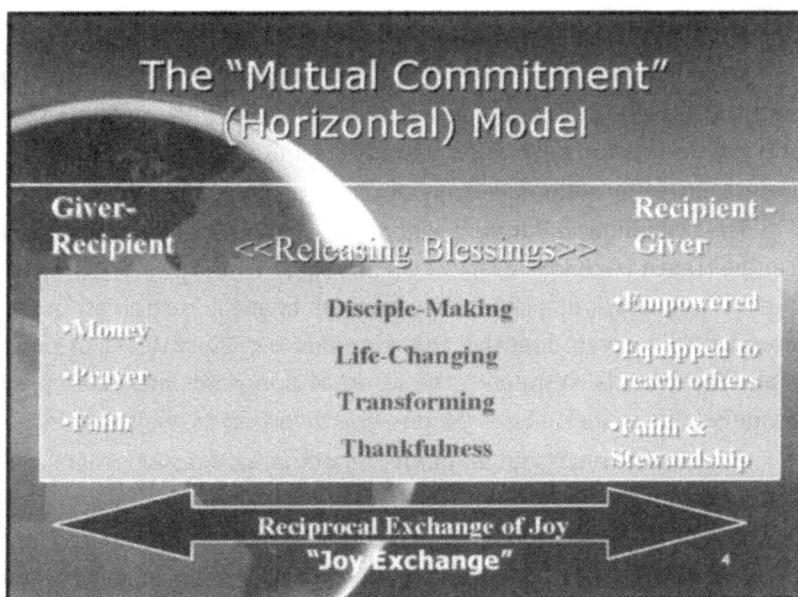

This new model can best be understood in the reorientation of five key concepts within giving and receiving: stewardship, relationship, accountability, dependency, and the role of intermediaries, *including the governance board* of an organization, college, university, seminary, local congregation, or not-for-profit ministry organization.

Our relationship must never be defined by—nor become limited to—the ritual and discipline of tithing, the mechanisms of financial transfers. Relationship value reflects the Body of Christ, not some economic standard or potential

Implementing the "Mutual Commitment" Model

The ultimate question asked by the Lausanne Issue Group on "Funding Evangelism and the Mission" was *How does the new model make funding the mission and vision more efficient and effective?* If the theological base for the new model is correct, as board members and those who manage God's resources here on earth mature in stewardship and expand the grace of giving, there will be ample resources for any project God desires to see accomplished. He is not short of funds—just short of mature stewards. Humanly, it may seem that His decision to trust His creation to channel His resources into investments that accomplish His goals is questionable.

That plan, like all of creation, has suffered immensely from the impact of the entry of sin into His creation. Once His creatures became distorted in values and priorities, their use of His creation also suffered. If the management of resources can be redeemed, the use of those resources will be re-channeled into His priorities.

Pragmatically, the questions are as follows:

- How does the local church board manage the tithes given, or the organization build a fund development program that accomplishes the "mutual benefit" design?
- How does the mature donor exercise the grace or gift of giving in such a way that the ministry is moved to the new model?

The crush of ministry budgets and the pressure of general funds war against the transitions necessary to reflect the characteristics of reciprocal blessings between donor and receiver. For decades the donor or "tither" has been seen as simply the supplier of funds. Furthermore, for decades donors have taken a rather passive attitude toward issues of ministry outside the consistent request for more funds. Out of excess comes that which meets the needs of those in ministry who have no excess. Consequently, there is no mutual growth relationship assumed or generated for the majority of donors other than that reflected in the level of financial participation.

Several steps should be considered as the school, church, or Christian organization makes a commitment to building a mutually beneficial fund development and financial management program.

1. Mailing lists, those cold and impersonal lists of names and addresses, may be categorized or stratified differently than by giving experience or potential. If there were a way to identify maturity of giving motivation or level of growth in the grace of giving, those categories would be much more conducive to knowing how best to communicate with mutual blessing than the size of the checkbook. Other categories, such as type of

ministry that interests the donor or level of personal involvement with the ministry, would assist in communications more mutually beneficial than the emotive plea for funds.

2. Communications designed specifically for various members of the family may assist in inviting those other than the checkwriter. Likewise, specific communications to various professional groupings may provide information useful for stimulating the involvement of those professionals in ministry.

3. Reducing the use of exploitive and emotionally manipulative stories and pictures without sterilizing the message may, over a period of time, provide a more accurate picture of ministry than is generated by extreme direct mail. Such a pattern of printed material would help preserve the dignity of those funded in needy parts of the world.

4. Patterns of communication that include more personal interaction, group meetings, conferences, mission trips, and so on will elevate the tither or donor from "source of money" to "partner in ministry."

5. Opportunity for tithers and donors to know the challenges as well as the blessings within a ministry will provide a foundation of reality for the donors as they give and pray.

6. Accurate reporting, rather than exaggerated numbers, will encourage respect for and identity with the normal challenges of ministry. A donor funding a "quick fix" to a massive problem will ultimately be disappointed and cynical about ministry.

7. While an organization, church, or school is legally accountable to its governing board, a spirit of accountability to the faithful givers and its supporting family would encourage maturity in that family. This is not a simple task. With diverse backgrounds and levels of maturity in the supporting family, the process of being accountable becomes very complex. Yet the organization that relates to its constituency in a comprehensive accountability pattern will develop strength in that "family." When members of the supporting family assist in the design

of accountability communication, the process becomes less threatening and more "joy-filled."

8. While the emotive dimension of life opens the door to funding decisions, it is the cognitive that builds maturity in all dimensions of life. The information shared between tither or donor, the intermediary, or board and receiver or recipient should be structured in such a way that it moves both giver and receiver to a higher level of trust relationship and cognitive connection. The donor needs to be prompted in stewardship growth and ministry awareness. The receiver should consistently refine efforts to both manage and report on the management of God's resources extended to the ministry. Stagnating the donor at the emotive level of involvement is a misuse of the stewardship trust.

Summary

The Lausanne Issue Group on Funding Evangelism and the Mission recommended a radical shift in the perspective of ministry organizations, including local churches and Christian colleges, toward funding principles. A fund development program, principled on biblical truths, has the potential of freeing God's resources from the tyranny of natural human inclination. The issues of funding have more to do with stewards than with money, more to do with stewardship maturity than matching dollars to budget projections. The ultimate availability of funds to accomplish God's Great Commission is not limited by quantity of resources but by the lack of quality of values and priorities within God's stewards that distort His intentions for effective mobilization of His wealth.

As we work on ministry boards of governance, we steadfastly focus on the mission, vision, and values of the organization, school, or local church. Remember: "generosity" means much more than "bigness" of amounts of money given. Rather, from a biblical perspective it refers to a quality of spirit and attitude reflected in both givers and receivers. Both donors and recipients must guard their attitudes and spirits as they serve as role models of generosity and stewardship.

Role Models of Generosity: Application

Local Church

"I want my tithe back, and then I'll leave the church." That's what the man said to me after a conversation in which I refused to let him dominate the church in general and worship services in particular.

Finance is often a source of contention within a local church. The challenges LeBron identifies are real.

The challenge of a shortage of funding for vision advancement seems to be present in most churches. Pastors need to remember that money is raised through credibility and integrity. You can increase your credibility and integrity by telling people what you know *and* what you don't know. People will not give if they do not trust the leadership. Integrity matters in fundraising.

The challenge of misusing funds has plagued some churches. Church leadership must, absolutely must, establish an acceptable accounting system, build in checks and balances, and generate and distribute finance reports in order to avoid financial mismanagement. I am often amazed at how this fact is overlooked or ignored: you must use funds for the purpose for which they were donated. Funds cannot be redirected to another purpose without the express written consent of the donor.

The challenge of distorting biblical principles is common. Here's the key: Remember that God owns everything. Everything belongs to God. We are simply stewards. The mistake often made by churches and donors alike is to think that the money is theirs rather than God's. It all belongs to God.

"I want my tithe back," insisted the church member.

"I'm sorry," I said. "You gave it to God, and He's already spent it."

Not-for-Profit Organization

As the last guests were leaving, one lady remarked, "That was a wonderful evening," and it was. The event was a gala produced by the community for the benefit of a local Christian not-for-profit organization. As we drove home that evening, it occurred to me just how wonderful the evening was—for many reasons. The significant amount of money raised would certainly be helpful, but more important, it confirmed the credibility the not-for-profit had built and maintained in the community over a number of years. Also, many of those present were directly involved in the ministry, and even a number of recipients of the ministry attended. It proved, once again, that *integrity matters.*

Funding for the operational needs of the not-for-profit organization is always on the minds of the board and leadership. The organization must "live within its means," yet there are always more needs that "somebody should meet." This poses a constant tension in the hearts and minds of caring Christian leaders who are exposed daily to unmet needs. How can this be resolved?

First, the effective not-for-profit board and staff must remain focused on their God-given mission and vision. Each organization is called to do only what the Father asks of it. Ministry pressures that move us away from His guidance result in burnout. This can and must be avoided. Seeking His will in the pursuit of ministry involves much prayer and at times fasting. The effective not-for-profit board member is committed to that kind of prayer life.

Second, the effective not-for-profit board increasingly approaches funding the organization more like "the mutual commitment"— the horizontal model LeBron describes in this chapter and less like the vertical model. Effective board members truly believe, as this chapter states, "all parties are on an equal plane, and all believers enjoy an equal standing before the throne of Christ." Personal interaction with financial partners is vital to assessing stewardship maturity and providing proper accountability. R. Scott Rodin and Gary G. Hoag in their book *The Sower* state, "Christian resource-raising is not solely about securing transactions or gifts; rather, it is about encouraging spiritual transformation that helps people become givers rich toward God (Foreword)."

Third, and most important, the effective not-for-profit board member is a genuine Christian model of generosity. Biblical stewardship is the only reliable guide. The Father will decide what the number of dollars should be. Ken Blanchard and S. Truett Cathy in their book *The Generosity Factor* have the character "Executive" state, "The success-motivated person tends to measure his or her life in terms of money, power, status, achievement, and recognition. The significant person places emphasis on a more spiritual view of life-generosity, empowerment of others, service, building up others, and helping them develop solid relationships" (p. 64). Significance over success is the Christian model of generosity. I believe Christian commitment is being redefined today: a major part of which deals with His ownership and our stewardship of financial resources.

Higher Education

Several years ago I spent a number of months on a seminary campus outside North America teaching and working with the school president in creating the development office of the seminary. Near the end of my assignment at the school, I shared with the esteemed leader some thoughts about his board and some recommendations related to the strengthening of the institutional advancement, or financial development administrative unit, of the institution.

I shared with him that "A strong and effective board of trustees is imperative if the seminary is to survive. The seminary could become the glue that holds the region together, theologically and denominationally. In fact, it could emerge as the centerpiece of regional strategy not just for the educational institutions on the region but also for the regional mission strategy itself."

I continued: "The region and the global Church of the Nazarene need the seminary leadership and the Board of Trustees to re-envision and re-position the seminary as 'The pre-eminent graduate level institution in the Wesleyan Holiness tradition for ministerial and mission education in the region and Southern Hemisphere.'"

I then shared the following recommendations with the president regarding institutional advancement and a financial development office on campus.

Recommendations

1. Strengthen relationships and clarify decision-making processes between the regional office leadership, field strategy coordinator, seminary leadership, and the Board of Trustees.

2. Develop the seminary gift processing manual and gift receipt letter plan.

3. Assign a full-time person to institutional advancement, and consider placing enrollment management, financial development, alumni relations, public relations, seminary communications, and regional office coordination within this unit.

4. Develop a no-more-than-five-minute video on the seminary and a new brochure for use with multiple constituents and for use at the seminary partnership meetings, especially at the General Assembly partnership breakfast.

5. Create a web page on the seminary home page on the "Approved Specials" building projects with appropriate visuals to illustrate needs and projected plans.

6. Create a four-fold color brochure highlighting the seminary's twenty-fifth-anniversary major building projects and endowment funds, and translate text into the major languages used by the Church of the Nazarene on the region.

7. Develop a computer program and upgrade the seminary donor list, including names of as many seminary Work-and-Witness team members as possible.

8. Create a board standing policies manual to clarify and strengthen the role of the seminary and processes needed to govern effectively as efficiently as possible, acknowledging the geographic diversity and distance of board members from the main campus.

9. Submit a request to the "Extreme Nazarenes" group to embrace the Evangelism and Education Building Initiative as a project for them to complete.

10. Make completion of the library a top priority in the development of the Evangelism and Education Center with a request to major donors and districts for funds to complete construction and build-out of the floor. Plan to dedicate the library in conjunction with the Board of Trustees meeting and commencement service.

11. Secure a full-time volunteer to serve as special assistant to the seminary president for administration.

12. Launch the International School of Communication in conjunction with the 25th anniversary celebration on campus with a twelve-month campaign to fund a $50,000 student endowment fund.

Richard Wood stated at a Council of Independent College National Workshop that "A strong board of governance will have members who understand their roles and the roles of others, will have the information it needs to govern and deal with ambiguities, and avoid dictating simple solutions to complex problems." He continued: "A strong board can also help the president be a risk-taker and to push against institutional inertia." He concluded, "The ability [of strong boards] to take risks without judgment provides deep freedom."

It is imperative for every board member to become a role model of generosity and stewardship and encourage those who are watching him or her to participate also. Amen! Board members who are generous in spirit and expansive in vision will set the pace in giving not just their own advice but also sacrificial financial gifts. These board members become the cheerleaders for and encouragers to the school leaders as they advance these initiatives and take the necessary risks to make the God-inspired dreams come true.

12

Pass It On

Jim Couchenour

Best Practice: Board members develop new leaders throughout the region for increased responsibilities and commitment to the organization.

I don't remember the setting. The location, date, time, and persons involved are completely lost to me. But I will never forget the serious impact with which these penetrating questions struck me. The questioner in a serious tone of voice said, "So the question is *What are the five most important decisions you've made in your life?* or put another way, *What five decisions have most impacted your life?* and *If you could change them, would you?*"

I fidgeted in my chair and quickly thought through the stages of my life and the accompanying decisions. Giving my life to God, marrying Pat, moving to Ohio, deciding to have children, becoming deeply involved in my church, starting a business. Then it occurred to me: without a doubt one of the most important human decisions in my life was made by someone else. This wasn't quite in line with the questioner's question, but it triggered a new realization for me. The human decision that most impacted the direction of my life was one made by my father, long before I could speak or write the word "decision." Prior to making that decision, Dad's lifestyle was by all accounts leading him, and therefore his family, in a direction diametrically opposed to God and godly living. On one revival night in a little Methodist church in Lowber, Pennsylvania, Dad met Jesus Christ, and his life was changed—radically changed—from the inside out.

From that moment he began to serve Jesus, and he did so for the remainder of his life and taught his family to do the same. The trajectory of my life was largely set by his decision. Dad passed his faith on to my brothers and sister and me and taught us to pass our faith on to our children. His family is now into the fourth generation of Christ-followers. One man "passed it on" and changed the world for his descendants, including me.

Good board members fulfill a role as essential for their organization as the one my dad fulfilled for his family. This role of being, doing, and passing it on is as crucial to an organization as a father's is to his family. Generations will experience the benefits. Persons unborn will benefit from it.

The principle of *passing it on* has existed throughout history. It is on display throughout the chronicles of civilizations and most important, in Scripture. Countless examples are given to us, such as those of Abraham and Isaac, Moses and Joshua, Mordecai and Esther, Paul and Timothy, and, of course, Jesus and the disciples.

To nurture future leadership is incumbent on every leader of every organization. For board members it means to intentionally mentor and nurture the next generation of board leaders. A good board member takes this role seriously. Several concepts are involved in completing this task.

Good board members are passionate advocates for the organization.

In their interaction with the organization's world, good board members tell its story. They protect it. They use their personal influence to further its causes. There is no question in the minds of their associates about their belief in and commitment to the organization.

Good board members are passionate advocates, because they are passionate about the organization and its mission and vision.

Their passion comes from deep within and is built into their hearts and minds. They care about what the organization does, how it is does its work, and what the results are of its existence in the world. Its success in fulfilling its mission and achieving its vision matters to them. If they have a question about an issue, they go to the person who can resolve it and work through it together. They know the world needs this organization. They are deeply convinced that God birthed it, sustains it, and cares about its mission and vision. They know it exists for His glory.

Good board members reproduce themselves as passionate advocates for the organization.

Good board members understand the importance of the past. Bob Cooley in his Board of Trustees Seminar at Nazarene Theological Seminary, October 28, 2010, said, "Once an institution loses its heritage, it is open to current winds of change." Good board members see the importance of connecting the heritage of the organization, its current mission, and their personal passion for both to today's emerging leaders. Guided by that motivation, they intentionally seek to reproduce themselves as passionate advocates for the organization.

They understand this to be a privilege that is uniquely theirs as a member of the board, and they respond to that opportunity as an integral part of being a board member.

Good board members nurture future leadership.

Good board members also understand the importance of the future. They know future leadership is vital to the success of the organization. They see themselves charged with responding to today's issues within the context of their heritage and with a watchful eye cast toward the future.

They understand the importance of passing the mantle of leadership on to others. So they pass it on by intentionally nurturing future leadership. They understand this opportunity to be a unique privilege of theirs to carry forward the leadership of the past and today.

As we analyze what it means to nurture future leadership and the processes involved, several important actions that are required to do it well come to mind.

Prayer. As with everything in God's kingdom, prayer must come first. Seeking God's guidance is imperative; the stakes are too high to rely on human judgment alone. As Andrew Murray stated, "We . . . regard it [prayer] as the highest work entrusted to us and as the root and strength of all other work" (Murray, *The Believer's School of Prayer*, p. 7). Certainly the starting point is listening to the Father.

Selection. A well-planned, active recruitment effort to attract top-quality young leaders will pay dividends to a board for years to come. In seeking new board members, finding leadership capability is always basic. Look deeply within the person for that nebulous but recognizable leadership potential. In one board's recent quest for a new president, the board was advised to read the résumés but then throw them away: then look for the personal characteristics that really matter. Three important observations on personal characteristics should be considered—

- Integrity is essential to leadership. Without integrity, everything else matters little. Remember the Packer Thomas Certified Public Accountants & Business Consultants motto: "In the long run integrity is the only thing that matters; indeed, if there is no integrity, there will not be a long run."
- A teachable spirit is important. Is the person willing to be led in development of his or her potential? Is the person willing to be led by the Lord? And is he or she willing to be led by you?
- Acceptance of responsibility is mandatory. Does the person accept personal responsibility for what happens? One family's motto, "When we blame others we forfeit the right to self-improvement," holds true in all situations.

Vision: As the mission and vision are shared with prospective board members, do they comprehend and accept them willingly and enthusiastically? Will they *own* them? Are they creative enough to expand and grow them? It has been said that passion is first, understanding is second, and creativity is third.

Modeling: As we fulfill our responsibilities well, they are inspired to do the same. As we provide them an example of what to do and how to do it, growth will occur. At this point it is important to mention that modeling generosity as described in chapter 11 is vital.

Teaching: Relevant information and learning materials such as a referenced list will provide important guidance to a potential leader.

Orientation and integration information such as the referenced list will be helpful for new board members.

Training: One good idea is to use committee work as a way to provide opportunities for emerging leaders to take on more responsibilities. Participation as a member of a committee will give exposure to the issues and an opportunity to observe the process and watch leaders at work. As additional responsibility is given to an emerging leader in committee work, he or she will have the opportunity to develop his or her leadership capacity and style. For balanced development, both cognitive and experiential learning are essential. A regular review of what is being learned is beneficial. Participation in committee work provides an opportunity to accomplish growth.

Within the committee structure, delegation of responsibility may be given in stages. *The Small Business Report* describes five levels of delegation with increasing responsibility and authority at each level, as follows:

1. Investigates and reports findings.
2. Investigates, presents alternative solutions, and recommends an action.
3. Investigates, recommends an action, and after approval initiates action.
4. Investigates, makes the decision, initiates action, and provides periodic feedback.
5. Investigates, makes the decision, takes the required actions, and reports the final results (Small Business Report, December 1982, p. 24).

These levels of delegation, or variations thereof, are useful in the training process

Structure: Nurturing future board leadership is of such vital importance to the organization that it is wise to include it as a significant component of the organization's strategic planning. Anticipating the future needs of the organization and clarifying the gifts and graces required to meet those needs are important considerations. Thoughtful planning is required.

For the same reasons, the nurturing of board leadership should be an integral part of the board development program and periodic assessment of the board.

Summary

The success of an organization across generations depends greatly on early and continuous planning for succession. Board members of today who understand the heritage of the organization are passionate advocates for it, see the future and reproduce themselves as passionate advocates, and then nurture future leaders—these are indispensable to the success of the organization.

Pass It On: Application

Local Church

There are many voices today that cry out a warning to the church. The warning is that many of our younger generations are walking away from the church. This should cause us to drop to our faces before the Lord in prayer, begging Him to teach us how to mentor and to give us wisdom to reach the younger generations.

Church leadership can be proactive in this endeavor by establishing a system of "passing it on." Goals that are systemic have a higher probability of being accomplished and lasting.

A component of this system is continual leadership development. Train, teach, develop—constantly. It is vital.

Another component I have used along with many other churches is a rotational system of leadership. Leaders rotate in and out of positions and leadership roles. One caution is to be careful that the rotations not become so long that you miss generations or not become so short that you establish no coherency in leadership. There are many models from which a church can choose.

Passing it on must permeate the life, heart, and mind of the church. Older leaders must intentionally target younger leaders for development.

My grandmother gave $1,000 to the church I pastored in 1984 for its building project. She was the widow of a farmer and funds were tight. When she gave the money she said to me, "I want to give my money to something that will outlast me." My grandmother is in heaven today. The church is alive and well. Pass it on.

Not-for-Profit Organization

"Passing it on" is vital to every organization's future. It is especially so in the not-for-profit world, because many not-for-profits are stand-alone organizations. Often there is no natural pool from which to draw future board members. The effective not-for-profit board member accepts the passing-it-on role as one of the most important privileges and responsibilities of service as a board member.

To pass it on is both a personal and board issue.

On the personal side, the effective board member models what an effective board member is and does. There is no substitute for authentic modeling. Passion for the organization and its mission and the privilege of serving on its board will, of itself, draw potential board members.

A model board member—

—is a passionate advocate for the not-for-profit.

—knows the nine functions of the board, the mission, vision, and values of the organization and makes decisions based on them.

—asks questions and follows the policies written in the Board Standing Policies Manual.

—watches his or her words, speaks with the board as one voice, is a person of integrity.

—takes time to think about issues, is open to missional change, assesses the organization's progress, and is a role model of generosity.

—is committed to intentionally seeking others inside and outside the organization to whom the passion can be passed on. (Many outstanding board members were originally recipients of the not-for-profit's services.)

—intentionally nurtures new board members.

On the board side, the effective not-for-profit board—

—facilitates an ethos in which "passing it on" is highly valued.

—develops a list of attitudes and qualifications of prospective board members.

—develops systems and policies to keep the search for the right prospective board members at the forefront of the board's agenda.

—develops strong orientation and training programs and materials for new board members.

—begins both the personal and board sides of seeking and training new leaders with prayer. Again, as Andrew Murray has stated in his classic book, *The Believer's School of Prayer*, ". . . prayer is not only the highest work to which we are called, it is the root and strength of all the other work. . . ." Finding the board members God wants for the not-for-profit organization He has commissioned is certainly "high work."

Higher Education

The method of selecting board members in Church of the Nazarene higher education institutions varies significantly from region to region. For some schools, ex-officio members dominate the board. For others, districts on the region elect trustees to the regional college, university, or seminary at their district assemblies in accordance with the institutions' bylaws.

Increasingly, districts are seeking advice from the school president and board chairperson regarding the selection process of trustees from the districts. At-large members are often elected by the school board in an effort to provide balance of gender, race, competencies, and skills.

At the request of a district superintendent in North America, the board leadership and school administration shaped the following principles to help achieve the election of credible, capable, and committed representatives for the district(s) to the board of governance.

Trustee Nomination

A suitable candidate for trustee emerges from the business of the institution:

1. Alumni: graduates who have a vested personal interest in its preservation and progress.

2. Pastors: persons who reflect and promote the primary values of the school in life and in leadership.

3. Business persons: those with valuable managerial and financial experience who lend credibility and support.

4. Professional services persons: public servants (doctors, lawyers, accountants, etc.) who bring the perspective of service and professional development.

5. Educators: leaders in the educational enterprise who provide insight and confirmation to the peculiarities of academic administration.

Trustee Qualifications

The characteristics of a trustee are shaped by the nature of the institution:

1. A person of integrity and principle, with credibility and influence among his or her peers.

2. Appropriate educational experience and degree(s) to provide sufficient background for effective decision-making.

3. A clear idea of the difference between policy-making and administrative work.

4. A general understanding of one or more of the following: funding development, construction, legal, and personnel concerns.

5. The skills to communicate the mission of the institution and to work collaboratively to achieve it.

6. The ability to think conceptually and responsibly regarding immediate and long-range issues.

7. Energy and credibility to help move the institution forward and upward in its scope and influence.

Trustee Motivation

The reasons for being a trustee are defined by the character of the institution:

1. An appreciation and concern for the role of Christian higher education in developing human potential.

2. An understanding of the importance of the integration of faith and learning to the vitality and growth of the church.

3. A passion for the mission of the school and an embrace of its vision and values.

4. A heart for students and a dedication to those who serve them.

5. Energy and creativity to help move the institution forward and upward in its scope and influence.

Trustee Expectations

The obligations of a trustee flow from a commitment to the institution and the church it serves:

1. Trustees can expect to devote significant time to the institution by—

—attending three plenary meetings each year, consistent with the bylaws of the institution.

—participating in committee and task force assignments.

—soliciting philanthropic support.

2. Trustees should expect to provide their best judgment to the board by—

—visiting the campus periodically and interacting with its various sectors.

—studying reports and developing/refining insights for strategic planning.

—staying aware of the external environment through dialogue and soliciting input from the context in which the school is working.

3. Trustees should be strongly supportive of the institution by—

—placing the institution as a top volunteer commitment.

—looking after the "care and feeding" of the president and his or her team.

—participating financially within his or her means as God leads.

4. Trustees can expect to gain personally and professionally from their relationship to the university by—

—becoming a friend of the campus and a custodian of its values.

—receiving valuable experience and training from board involvement.

—feeling the affirmation from seeing the fruit of one's labor in the smiles of young people prepared to make a difference in the world with the love of Christ

Adapted from *What Every Trustee Should Know* by Robert Peck.

The President's Foundation for the Support of Higher Education, 1996:

Board members search for potential members of the board and make recommendations accordingly and appropriately. These individuals are often "discovered" on ad hoc committees of the board, on local church and community boards, and from presentations made at the local, regional, or national level. Our goal is to "pass on" to another generation our energy, love, commitment, and passion for the higher education institution on whose board we are privileged to serve.

Postscript

As a leader I have served as pastor, not-for-profit director, and I have completed a PhD in Education in the field of leadership for higher education. In many regards, I have more varied experience and have been more educated than many of my peers. Still, I have attended my share of bad board meetings, I have served on boards that suffered from a lack of clarity and direction, boards that were ineffective and aimless, and boards that were okay but could have been better.

Many leaders believe that real board development is expensive and therefore reserved only for big companies or organizations with high profile consultants, and is more show than substance. The local church board, not-for-profit Christian organization, and the Christian higher education board of governance have existed on good intentions and prayer for years with no apparent need to change that perspective. The common thought was that board proceedings were run according to Robert's Rules of Order to control the chaos, and that was enough to guide the meetings.

When I found myself sitting in a room with these three gifted leaders as they began to develop this book, I realized how little I knew about boards, governance, and the need for board development.

The process of working with the writers and their material has transformed my thinking about governance and the continual, systematic need for legitimate board development. Through this thoughtfully developed resource, which draws from their years of experience, board development has become practical and approachable for even the smallest board.

I have never encountered a more concise and practical guide for board development. Relevant, compelling, life-changing, and sustaining on both an individual and board level, *Best Practices for Effec-*

tive Boards will challenge your board to become the most effective, God-honoring body to ever serve your organization. Regardless of the size of your board or the organizations you serve, you can benefit from the principles outlined in this book. The starting point is clear, and the path is laid out in a way that by working on these best practices at each board meeting, no matter where you start, you can develop your board into a strong and effective board with a culture toward a future of growth and development.

The underlining passion of these men that I have come to appreciate—the one concept that permeates and is between the lines of every page—is that as one serves an organization as a member of the board or as the organization's leader, as a follower of Christ, integrity matters.

Tammy Condon

APPENDIX 1
For This We Stand

Values Underlying the Mount Vernon Nazarene University Faith Community

Throughout the past few months I have been asking myself some fundamental questions: (1) What drives or motivates Mount Vernon Nazarene College as a Christian college of higher education? (2) What characterizes us at our best and convicts us at our worst? (3) What shapes the lifestyle—the words, action, and behavior—of a faith community? (4) What is foundational to our conviction that God calls all believers to a life of holiness? (5) What are the values for which we stand?

The biblical mandate for the holy life, I affirmed, is summed up in the scriptural commands to "love the Lord thy God with all thy heart, soul, mind and strength, and thy neighbor as thyself" (Deuteronomy 6:5; Leviticus 19:18; Matthew 22:37-40; Mark 12:30-31, KJV).

The one thing Spirit-filled Christians "will" to do is summarized in the holistic command and commitment to love God, respect others, and take responsibility for self with all our heart, soul, mind, and strength.

I concluded after much prayer and reflection that the values affirmed and foundational to the MVNC faith community (faculty, staff, and students) are grounded in the biblical mandate for the holy life, grounded in the rich Judeo-Christian tradition.

A. Affirmation #1: WE LOVE GOD. Therefore, we value and stand for
   1. A Worshiping Community
   2. A Biblical Faith
   3. A Christlike Lifestyle

4. A Holiness Ethic
5. A Global Mission
6. A Creation Vision
7. A Spirit-Empowered Devotion

B. Affirmation #2: WE RESPECT OTHERS. Therefore, we value and stand for

1. A Magnanimous Spirit
2. A Servant Mentality
3. A Trustworthy Character
4. A Positive Influence
5. A Courteous Response
6. A Giving Motivation
7. An Appreciative Attitude

C. Affirmation #3: WE ARE RESPONSIBLE FOR OURSELVES. Therefore, we value and stand for

1. An Inquisitive Mind
2. A Disciplined Schedule
3. Modest Attire
4. A Balanced Diet
5. A Physical Fitness Commitment
6. A Reliable Word
7. A Lifelong Learning and Growth Perspective

To read the entire article, go to www.BoardServe.org/writings/ where this article is located. *For This We Stand* is number one under "Recently Published Books, Essays/Manuscripts."

Leader Effectiveness Review[*]

Higher Education Senior Administrator, Faculty, and Staff

In an attempt to be faithful stewards of the leadership assignment given education leaders in the Church of the Nazarene, the following review process for each leader is provided. The term "leaders" is used to refer to the school president/principal/vice chancellor of a Church of the Nazarene college, university, or seminary. The instrument may be modified for the school leader to use with administrators who serve with the school leader. Fundamental to the nature of this review process is mutual dialogue between the leader and the board of governors to whom the person being reviewed reports. This is a critical component of the review process.

The review has three sections. Sections one and three are to be completed by the school leader prior to the official leader effectiveness review meeting. Section two is to be completed by the board of governors committee appointed to oversee the review process prior to the official review of the college, university, or seminary leader or the supervisor of the leader. The "Competency Grid" in section two may be used by the review committee chairperson or supervisor to facilitate the discussion of the response in section two.

The date for the review will be set by committee chairperson, in consultation with the school leader, and review member participants. The committee chairperson will determine if a meeting of the review committee without the school leader is necessary. If so, the leader will be briefed on the executive session.

I. Reflections/Projections *(to be answered by the school leader)*
1. How does your specific assignment support the overarching mission and vision of the institution you serve and the Church of the Nazarene? Provide some examples.

2. Has your sense of calling and personal ministry been fulfilled through your leadership endeavors? If not, why? If so, how? Do you feel affirmed as a valuable asset? If not, why? If so, how?

3. In what ways have you developed and enhanced your job knowledge and performance? Have adequate opportunities been provided both for training and for personal growth since your last review/evaluation? Please give examples.

4. What specific tasks or accomplishments during the past four years best express your commitment to high-quality service and servant leadership to school constituents, including evangelism, discipleship training, leadership development, fiscal management, and vision-casting? How have your gifts and talents been most effectively used?

5. In what ways have your initiatives contributed to the numerical growth and spiritual development of the institution you serve? What additional resources might assist you as your strive to strengthen your school?

6. How can the climate of collaboration within the school and with other schools be enhanced?

7. In what ways can the board of governance support you to lead more effectively?

8. What are your three top institutional challenges for the next year? The next four years? What short-term and long-term goals have you established for your assignment in light of these challenges? How will you know when your goals have been reached?

9. Are your short-term and long-term goals aligned with the institution's strategic plan? Please give examples.

II. Evaluation of the school leader based upon the following "Convictions of a Christian Leader"

(To be completed by the Board of Governors Review Committee and/or supervisor of the school leader)

Convictions of a Christian Leader

1. Speak gracefully. *Watch the words you speak.*
2. Live gratefully. *Don't whine; be grateful.*
3. Listen intently. *Seek first to understand.*

4. Forgive freely. *Be proactive in extending forgiveness.*

5. Lead decisively. *Combine deep humility with fierce resolve.*

6. Care deeply. *Value people, not power.*

7. Pray earnestly. *Pray for change in you even as you pray for change in others.*

Instructions: *Circle the number for each statement that most characterizes the school leader from 1 (never); 2 (seldom); 3 (occasionally); 4 (often); and 5 (always).*

1. The school leader uses words that serve to encourage others.

   1   2   3   4   5

2. The school leader gives gratitude to God and others as a fundamental lifestyle.

   1   2   3   4   5

3. People feel understood when communicating with the school leader.

   1   2   3   4   5

4. Forgiveness is requested by the school leader when colleagues or students are offended.

   1   2   3   4   5

5. A clear "vision" is embraced and articulated by the school leader.

   1   2   3   4   5

6. The prayers of the leader reflect a desire for personal change.

   1   2   3   4   5

7. Caring for personal and professional growth of colleagues is important to the school leader.

   1   2   3   4   5

8. Words spoken are culturally sensitive and consistent with actions taken by the school leader.

   1   2   3   4   5

9. Comparison to others (regions, districts, finances, talents, and so on) by the school leader is minimal.

   1   2   3   4   5

10. Honest and intense differences are accepted by the school leader.

   1   2   3   4   5

11. Resentment and bitterness are not harbored by the school leader.

   1   2   3   4   5

12. Prayer for colleagues, staff, and the ministry is frequent and evident.

   1   2   3   4   5

13. Responsibility for decision-making does not paralyze the school leader.

   1   2   3   4   5

14. The primary focus of the school leader is on plans and programs that unite, not divide.

   1   2   3   4   5

15. Colleagues feel blessed and affirmed in conversations and meetings with the school leader.

   1   2   3   4   5

16. The school leader brings out the "best" in others.

   1   2   3   4   5

17. People feel valued when discussing issues with the school leader.

   1   2   3   4   5

18. Extending forgiveness is convictional to the school leader.

   1   2   3   4   5

19. The school leader leads decisively in the midst of complex and difficult situations.

   1   2   3   4   5

20. The school leader values people, not power and position.

    1   2   3   4   5

21. The school leader leads with the conviction that some issues are resolved only through prayer and total dependence on God.

    1   2   3   4   5

Leading Decisively with Christian Humility

The ranking below is not an evaluation of past performance. Rather, it is a projection for the next four years.

Rank in order of priority *(1 = least important; 7 = most important)* the leadership skills that should be nurtured during the next four years.

____   Affirming and encouraging skills
____   Asking and listening skills
____   Conceptual and analytical skills
____   Financial management and budget development skills
____   "Strengths" discernment and delegation skills
____   Networking and communication skills
____   Timing and decision-making skills

III. Summary/Recommendations *(to be completed by the college/university/seminary leader)*

A. Provide a summary of your leadership strengths and how these are most effectively utilized in your ministry assignment as a school leader.

B. Provide a summary of your leadership limitations and how you plan to address these during the next four years.

Executive Session (if necessary):
Review/Evaluation Committee recommendation to the Board of Trustees:

*Used by permission of Board Serve LLC. BoardServe.org

Leader Effectiveness
Review Competency Grid*

Nazarene Higher Education Senior Administrators, Faculty, and Staff

*For use by the Board of Governance Review Committee
or the Supervisor of the Leader*
Use in analyzing responses to Section Two—Evaluation

Area of Competency	#	Leadership Behavior	Leader	Supervisor or Committee Chair	Comments or Suggestions
Speak Gracefully					
	1.	Words used serve to encourage others.			
	8.	Words are culturally sensitive and consistent with actions taken.			
	15.	Colleagues feel blessed and affirmed in conversations and meetings.			
Live Gratefully					

	2.	Gratitude to God and others is a fundamental lifestyle.
	9.	Comparison to others (regions, districts, finances, talents, and so on) is minimal.
	16.	Brings out the best in others.
Listen Intently		
	3.	People feel understood when communicating with the leader.
	10.	Honest and intense differences are accepted.
	17.	People feel valued when discussing issues.
Forgive Freely		
	4.	Forgiveness is requested when colleagues or students are offended.
	11.	Resentment and bitterness are not harbored.
	18.	Extending forgiveness is convictional to the leader.
Lead Decisively		
	5.	A clear "vision" is embraced and articulated.

Lead Decisively

5. A clear "vision" is embraced and articulated.

13. Responsibility for decision-making does not paralyze the leader.

19. Leads decisively in the midst of complex and difficult situations.

Care Deeply

7. Care is obvious for the personal and professional growth of colleagues.

14. The primary focus is on plans and programs that unite, not divide.

20. People are valued, not power and position.

Pray Earnestly

6. The leader's prayers reflect a desire for personal change.

12. Praying for others is witnessed, affirmed, and frequent.

21. Leads with the conviction that some issues are resolved only through prayer and total dependence on God.

Board Standing Policy Manual

Nazarene University
North America
(name omitted)

1.4 Board of Trustees Governance Structure and Process

The following descriptions of the university's governance structure and process are reproduced from the Board of Trustees' *Standard Policy* document.

1.4.1 General Statement on Governance

1. The university is a private higher education institution sponsored by the Church of the Nazarene. The Board of Trustees constitutes the school's Corporate Board, governs the university, and elects the university president.

2. The president, as the chief executive officer, directs and supervises all operations of the university in the implementation of its stated mission. The president is the chief spokesperson and representative of the institution, ultimately responsible for communications both internal to the university and external with the larger community.

3. The president ensures that governance policies are clearly articulated and implemented. The president appoints, after conferring with the Executive Committee, all senior administrators of the university, who report to the president on a regular basis and make reports to the Board of Trustees on occasion.

1.4.2 Principles of Governance

1. The ultimate responsibility for the university rests in its Board of Trustees. The board cannot delegate its fiduciary responsibility for the academic integrity, spiritual well-being, and financial

health of the institution. Traditionally, and for practical reasons, the board delegates some kinds of authority to other stakeholders with the implicit and sometimes explicit condition that the board reserves the right to question, challenge, and occasionally override decisions or proposals it judges to be inconsistent with the mission, integrity, or financial position of the university. For example, the delegation of authority to the administration and faculty in adding, reducing, or discontinuing academic programs is made with the implicit understanding that the board still retains the ultimate responsibility.

2. The Board of Trustees retains ultimate responsibility and full authority to determine the mission of the institution in consultation with, and on the advice of, the president in consultation with faculty, staff, and other key stakeholders. The board is also responsible for establishing the strategic direction of the institution through its insistence on, and participation in, comprehensive planning.

3. The board should conduct its affairs in a manner that exemplifies the behavior it expects of other participants in institutional governance. From time to time, the board should examine its structure and performance and should expect the same of faculty and staff.

   The board will avoid the temptation to micromanage in matters of administration. Board members will avoid even the perception of any personal or special interests. Board members will avoid undermining the administration.

4. Higher education governance is the responsibility of the Board of Trustees. The involvement of internal stakeholder groups—administrators, faculty, non-academic staff, and students—will vary according to subject matter and/or level of decision-making. The Board of Trustees is responsible for establishing the rules by which stakeholders' voices are considered and states explicitly who has the authority for what kinds of decisions—that is, to which persons or bodies it has delegated authority and whether that delegation is subject to board review. The board will insure that no single stakeholder group is given an exclusive franchise in any area, while recognizing that the subject matter in question

will determine which groups have primary or secondary responsibilities.

5. The board reserves the right to review and ratify specified academic decisions, as well as proposals to adopt major new academic programs or eliminate others. The board should set budget guidelines concerning resource allocation on the basis of assumptions, usually developed by the administration, that are widely communicated to interested stakeholders and subject to ample opportunity for challenge. Once the board makes these decisions, it should delegate resource-allocation decisions to the president, who may in turn delegate to others.

6. The university president is the board's major window on the institution, and the board should expect both candor and sufficient information from the president. In turn, the board should support the president while ensuring that the voices of other stakeholders are heard.

7. The Board of Trustees has the responsibility to appoint and assess the performance of the president.

8. No board member should favor any particular constituency or segment of the organization to the neglect of serving the institution as a whole.

1.4.3 Board of Trustees Responsibilities

The legal governing body for the university, the Board of Trustees, is composed of the university president and members elected by the church districts of the educational region plus two representatives from the alumni, and five at-large members elected by the board. The Board of Trustees is an autonomous body charged with the governance of the university, without legal control by the church constituency.

The annual meeting of the Board of Trustees is held in the fall consistent with the *ByLaws*. Two other meetings are normally held during the academic year, one at the time of commencement, as required by the *Bylaws*, and the other, a spring meeting, to consider the budget for the coming year. The Executive Committee is empowered by the *Bylaws* to act for the Board of Trustees in the interim between regular meetings. Since the board members reside within the educational region of the university, special meetings do not require major travel or other expenditures.

Duties and Responsibilities

The duties and responsibilities of the Board of Trustees include, but are not limited, to the following:

1. Elect the president, the chief executive officer of the university.

2. Upon recommendation of the president, approve the appointment of all administrative officers and faculty members.

3. Set forth the general policies of the university and make such rules, laws, and regulations as shall be deemed necessary for the governance of the university.

4. Approve the broad educational policies of the university, assuring that they achieve the stated mission and goals.

5. Approve policies concerning the financing, investment program, and business management of the university.

6. Review the annual audit of the financial accounts.

7. Give final approval to the promotion, demotion, or dismissal of faculty members.

8. With the president and other appropriate administrators, plan new buildings.

9. Approve policies concerning the management of buildings and grounds.

10. Review and approve the annual budget.

11. Approve tuition charges and fees.

12. Upon recommendation of the president, grant degrees and diplomas to candidates who have completed the required work.

13. Upon nomination by the president and the Honorary Degree Committee, approve and confer all honorary degrees.

14. Create and provide for all committees necessary to the work and administration of the corporation in accordance with the *Charter* and *Bylaws* of the corporation.

15. Hold title to all property of the corporation: real, mixed, and personal.

16. Perform all other duties of the affairs of the corporation and execute all powers and privileges conferred upon it by the *Articles of Incorporation*, the *Bylaws,* and the laws of the land.

Official communication lines between trustees and teaching personnel and staff shall be initiated only by the trustees or by the president.

The *Articles* and *Bylaws* constitute the legal documents under which the university is incorporated. Although the contents relate primarily to affairs of the Board of Trustees and the duties of administrative officers, certain sections are of interest to the faculty. Copies of these documents are filed in the president's office and the library.

17. Provide well-defined and clear channels of communication throughout the organizational structure of the university.

18. Provide dissemination of information about the university to its public.

19. Determine the eligibility requirements for leave of absence and/or sabbatical leave for personnel.

20. Be available for conferences with members of the administrative staff, faculty members, and students.

21. Nominate to the Board of Trustees candidates for honorary degrees who have been recommended by the Honorary Degree Committee.

22. Preside at meetings of the faculty.

23. Act as an agent through whom any communications from faculty to the board shall pass.

24. Represent the university at educational association meetings.

25. Plan and implement a program of instruction, research, and service to meet the needs of students.

26. Make an annual written report to the Board of Trustees.

27. Adopt regulations and procedures necessary to implement the policies established by the Board of Trustees.

28. Adopt regulations and procedures necessary to effectuate the duties and responsibilities delegated to the president.

29. Supervise university personnel.

30. Recommend the discipline and dismissal of university personnel.

31. Perform such other duties and functions as are necessary and appropriate from time to time or are delegated by the Board of Trustees.

32. Exercise such implied authority as is necessary and appropriate to the accomplishment of the responsibility and authority expressly granted to the president by the Board of Trustees.

1.5 Administrative Organization

1.5.1 President of the University

The president of the university is elected by the Board of Trustees of the university and is responsible and amenable only to the board. The president is the chief executive officer and is charged with full responsibility for the administration of affairs of the university in harmony with the Board of Trustees' decisions and the *Bylaws* of the corporation.

Duties and Responsibilities

The duties and responsibilities of the president include, but are not limited to, the following:

1. Serve as a member of the Board of Trustees.
2. Serve as a member of the Executive Committee of the Board of Trustees and consult with the board in the interim between meetings.
3. Guard the sacred honor and trust of the university set forth by the articles and bylaws of the corporation and the *Manual* of the Church of the Nazarene.
4. Recommend all faculty members for employment or renewal of contract to the Board of Trustees.
5. Recommend all administrative officers for employment and for renewal of contract to the Board of Trustees.
6. Appoint such other administrative officers and councils as deemed necessary to the operation of the educational work of the university.
7. Be responsible for faculty organization and development to provide effective instruction.
8. Approve the official university calendar, establishing beginning and ending dates and vacation periods.
9. After consultation with the Vice-president for Academic Affairs and school deans, locate candidates for the teaching staff and recommend to the Board of Trustees all appointments to the faculty.

10. After consultation with the Vice-president for Academic Affairs and the Faculty Rank Committee, recommend the academic rank of faculty members to the Board of Trustees.

11. Be responsible for the discipline of the university.

12. Be responsible for recruitment, enrollment, and supervision of qualified students.

13. Provide financial resources through an adequate development program including capital and operational budgets.

14. Provide for appropriate support services such as plant management, budgeting, accounting, auditing, purchasing, and financial reporting.

15. Sign all degrees and diplomas of graduation.

16. Be an ex officio member of all administrative and faculty committees.

17. Provide well-defined and clear channels of communication throughout the organizational structure of the university.

18. Provide dissemination of information about the university to its public.

19. Determine the eligibility requirements for leave of absence and/or sabbatical leave for personnel.

20. Be available for conferences with members of the administrative staff, faculty members, and students.

21. Nominate to the Board of Trustees candidates for honorary degrees who have been recommended by the Honorary Degree Committee.

22. Preside at meetings of the faculty.

23. Act as an agent through whom any communications from faculty to the board shall pass.

24. Represent the university at educational association meetings.

25. Plan and implement a program of instruction, research, and service to meet the needs of students.

26. Make an annual written report to the Board of Trustees.

27. Adopt regulations and procedures necessary to implement the policies established by the Board of Trustees.

28. Adopt regulations and procedures necessary to effectuate the duties and responsibilities delegated to the president.

29. Supervise university personnel.

30. Recommend the discipline and dismissal of university personnel.

31. Perform such other duties and functions as are necessary and appropriate from time to time or are delegated by the Board of Trustees.

32. Exercise such implied authority as is necessary and appropriate to the accomplishment of the responsibility and authority expressly granted to the president by the Board of Trustees.

1.5.2 University Organizational Structure

1.5.3 President's Administrative Cabinet

The President's Administrative Cabinet is composed of the president, the vice-presidents, and the Executive Assistant to the President for Planning, Institutional Research and Compliance. It deals with day-to-day issues, particularly matters of operations and procedures. It also acts as the sounding board for other areas. The cabinet serves as the crisis management team when necessary. The cabinet handles problems developing in the administrative divisions of the university. It also relates to the spiritual life of the campus family and to church/university relations. The cabinet may generate recommendations to the Board of Trustees or undergraduate/graduate academic councils. Cabinet meetings provide a time of sharing, keeping members informed, policy-making, and decision-making within parameters established by the Board of Trustees. The cabinet meets regularly according to a semester calendar or by the president's permission in the president's absence. See "Guiding Principles for Senior Administrators" in the president's office for additional information regarding the policies, processes, and procedures of the cabinet.

1.5.4 President's Advisory Council

The President's Advisory Council is composed of the president, who serves as chairperson of the council, a faculty member elected by the faculty, a staff member elected by the full-time staff, the Student Government Association president, and a student elected by the Student Government Association.

The council meets on call of the chairperson, but no less than once a semester. The council is not a decision-making body but is advisory in nature and can make recommendations to the various decision-making committees, including the President's Administrative Cabinet. The council serves as the communication link between the various groups on campus and the president on issues related to administrative concerns, policies, procedures, or personnel.

The President's Advisory Council discusses matters at the request of the president regarding general administration, organization or committee changes, university calendar, convocations, and other matters that the president refers to it. Agenda items can also be referred to the council in advance of the meetings through the elected representatives.

To be revised annually

APPENDIX 5
On Caring Enough to Confront

Conflict is what develops between individuals when they differ. David Augsburger in his book *Caring Enough to Confront* (Regal Books, 1981) says, "When your thrust as a person runs counter to mine, to deny my own thrust is to be untrue to the push and the pull of God within me."

Augsburger says, "Conflict is natural, normal and neutral. Conflict is neither good nor bad, right nor wrong. Conflict simply is. And how we view, approach and work through our differences does to a large extent determine our whole life pattern." The question is not "Will conflict arise?" The question is "How do we deal with it?"

Virginia Satir in her book *Peoplemaking* explains how we normally deal with conflict situations. Ninety-six percent of troubled families deal with conflict in one of four inappropriate ways (p. 78):
1. Placate (give in)
2. Blame
3. Compute
4. Distract (p. 59)

The result of using the four inappropriate ways is that the problem remains, tension mounts, and the relationship is edgy.

There is a fifth option—I care enough to confront" (Augsburger), "leveling with love" (Satir), or "Speak the truth in love" (see Ephesians 4:15).

Care-fronting or "leveling" as referred to by Augsburger is the biblical principal of "speaking the truth in love." This option brings healing, enables growth, and produces change, but only four percent of us deal with conflict in this manner. There are two arms of a genuine relationship — confrontation with truth and affirmation of love.

So how can I begin to manage conflict in a "caring and confronting" way? **First,** we must eliminate a win/lose mentality (I'm right—you're wrong). There are three methods of the win/lose mentality: I win—you lose (authoritarian); you win; I lose (permissiveness); no win (negativism).

Reaching out is two-sided, based on others' needs and our own needs. With the left hand reaching out—I do care; I want to respect you; I want your respect; and with the right hand reaching out—I want you to know how I feel; I want to tell you where I am; I have this goal for our relationship. This "caring and confronting" approach ends the blaming game, gets to healing questions—in simple, clear, direct language.

You must ask yourself, "Where do we start? What is the loving, responsible, truly respectful thing to do?, Where do we go from here?"

Trying to truly hear what another says—how it is said, what feelings are conveyed—is the art of "active listening." This practice involves hearing with an inner ear the feelings, hurts, angers, and demands of the other person.

Second, use "I" messages instead of "You" messages. "I" messages reflect my feelings without placing blame. "You" messages are most often attacks, criticisms, faultfinding of the other person, labels, and ways of fixing blame. There is a tremendous difference between an honest confessional ("I" message) and distorted rejection ("You" message).

Third, eliminate "why" questions. "Why" questions are an effective way of manipulating others (similar to "You" messages). (i.e. "Why do you always bring that issue up?" "Why don't *you* do something about it?" "Why don't you show a little compassion to the pastor?" "Why can't we get a little cooperation from you?") We use "why" questions to give hidden messages of anger that we are unwilling to own honestly. "Why" questions are like a "hit and run."

Fourth, we must give clear "yes" or "no" signals. "Yes" signals come easily; however, "no" signals come very hard—especially face-to-face. Often we hesitate to clearly state our feelings for fear of rejection/disapproval of others. Jesus said, "Let your 'yes' be a clear 'yes' and your 'no', 'no.'"

Fifth, we should initiate discussion if we have a complaint. Accept anger as a normal, natural human emotion. Clear statements of anger are something different than feelings and angry demands. Clear statements are a positive emotion, a self-affirming emotion that responds to the heart of rejection and devastation. There are two types of anger to consider—personal anger and virtuous anger, which is anger focused on the deed, not the person. Virtuous anger can slice through emotional barriers or communication barriers and establish contacts.

"Speaking the truth in love," or "truthing it in love," is the Christlike response to conflict.

It describes a lifestyle for Christians who care enough to confront where conflicts arise. Re-read Ephesians 4:15-32. When differences between people are dealt with openly, conflict can be a positive experience, because it can lead to personal growth. But when differences are concealed and individuals are prevented from expressing themselves, personal growth will not occur.

Personal conflict, in and out of board meetings, is a part of growing up, trying out new capabilities, and maturing as a Christian. Individually and collectively, we need to learn the value of expressing differences openly and listening to the other persons' response in the hope of reaching some sort of understanding.

IN CONFLICT MANAGEMENT
THE KEY ISSUE IS UNDERSTANDING, NOT AGREEMENT

Key questions to ask in the midst of conflict situations are—*What can I learn?* and *How can I change?* These are growth-producing questions. On the contrary, growth-inhibiting questions are—*Why me?* and *What if?* This is the could-have, should-have, would-have way of thinking. Following is a diagram of the two ways of thinking and reacting.

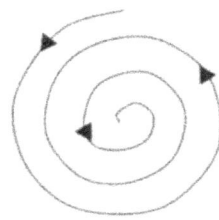

These two ways of thinking and reacting can be diagrammed

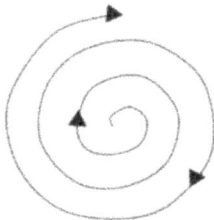

Growth-producing   Growth-inhibiting

APPENDIX 6

Rules of the Road for Christlike Communication

1. If you have a problem with someone, talk with him or her personally and privately.
2. If someone has a problem with another individual and comes to you, send him or her to that individual.
3. If someone consistently will not talk with the individual with whom he or she has a problem, say, "Let's go to the person together."
4. Be careful how you interpret other people. On matters that are unclear, do not feel pressured to interpret someone's feelings or thoughts. It is easy to misinterpret intentions if you are not sure.
5. If it's confidential, don't tell. (This especially applies to board meetings.) If anyone comes to you in confidence, don't tell unless
   - the person is going to harm himself/herself,
   - the person is going to physically harm someone else, or
   - a child has been physically or sexually abused.
6. Do not write or read unsigned letters or notes.
7. Do not manipulate others, and don't be manipulated.
8. When in doubt, just say it. The only dumb questions are those that aren't asked. We are a family, and we care about each other, so if you have a concern, pray, then (if led to do so) ask.

Rules of the Road for Christlike Conflict Management

The Role of the Pastor
- To name the name of God in the conflict
- To deal appropriately with sin (if involved)
- To proclaim truth in the midst of the conflict
- To enable people to come to grips with the conflict, seeing it in a biblical perspective and acting upon it in a manner consistent with the Bible.

The Role of Church Leaders
To be spiritual leaders as defined by the roles of priests, prophets, and equippers
- Priests—to help shepherd and guide the people; to be a healing agent
- Prophets—to speak the truth in love (even if it is confrontational)
- Equippers—to help people deal with the conflict

Guidelines for Christlike Behavior in the Midst of Conflict
- Sincerely seek the help of God in prayer.
- Seek to understand before we're understood.
- Engage in open, honest, direct, constructive communication.
- Seek for solutions once the issues are identified.
- Treat people as valuable.
- Address ideas and actions—do not attack people.

Scriptural Thoughts for Times of Conflict
- How good and pleasant it is when God's people live together in unity! (Psalm 133:1).
- I in them and you in me—so that they may be brought to complete unity. Then the world will know that you sent me and have loved them even as you have loved me (John 17:23).

- May the God who gives endurance and encouragement give you the same attitude of mind toward each other that Christ Jesus had, so that with one mind and one voice you may glorify the God and Father of our Lord Jesus Christ (Romans 15:5).
- Make every effort to keep the unity of the Spirit through the bond of peace (Ephesians 4:3).
- Over all these virtues put on love, which binds them all together in perfect unity (Colossians 3:14)

Rules of Engagement

Cogun, Inc.

A. Purpose

Trust is the currency of every team. Synergy is purchased through trust, and it's possible to have millions "in the bank" (powerful synergy) or be in significant debt (negative synergy). Trust is developed through the choices we make.

B. I choose to have the right attitude

1. I recognize that everyone has been created in the image of God and as such deserves my respect.
2. I will not be passive-aggressive or try to overpower others with emotion.
3. I believe that unhealthy things cannot grow in sunlight, so I will conduct all aspects of my relationships in the sunlight.
4. I will be proactive in all relationships with my team members.
5. I will take responsibility for clarity in expectations.
6. I will communicate honestly with team members using respectful language.
7. I will celebrate and consider the unique perspectives and contributions each team member brings.
8. I will listen and value what is said even though I may not agree.
9. I will be cooperative and look for ways I can help the team achieve common goals.

C. I Choose to be trustworthy

1. I commit to do what I say I will do, and when I don't, I'll tell you.
2. I commit to not over-promise and under-deliver. But if it looks as though that's where things are headed, I'll tell you.

3. If you confront me about the apparent gaps, I will tell you the truth.

4. I will keep sensitive information confidential.

5. I will avoid gossip or unfair criticism of others.

D. I choose to trust

1. When there are gaps between what I expect you to do and what you actually do, I will choose to close the gap with trust.

2. When I observe someone filling a gap with a suspicion, I will come to your defense.

3. If what I experience begins to erode my trust, I will come directly to you about it.

4. If we are not able to resolve the gap, we will involve a third party to help us resolve the gap.

Love is patient, love is kind. It does not envy, it does not boast, it is not proud. It is not rude, it is not self-seeking, it is not easily angered, it keeps no record of wrongs. Love does not delight in evil but rejoices with the truth. It always protects, always trusts, always hopes, always preserves (1 Corinthians 13:4-7).

If you are offering your gift at the altar and there remember that your brother has something against you, leave your gift there in front of the altar. First go and be reconciled to your brother; then come and offer your gift (Matthew 5:23-24).

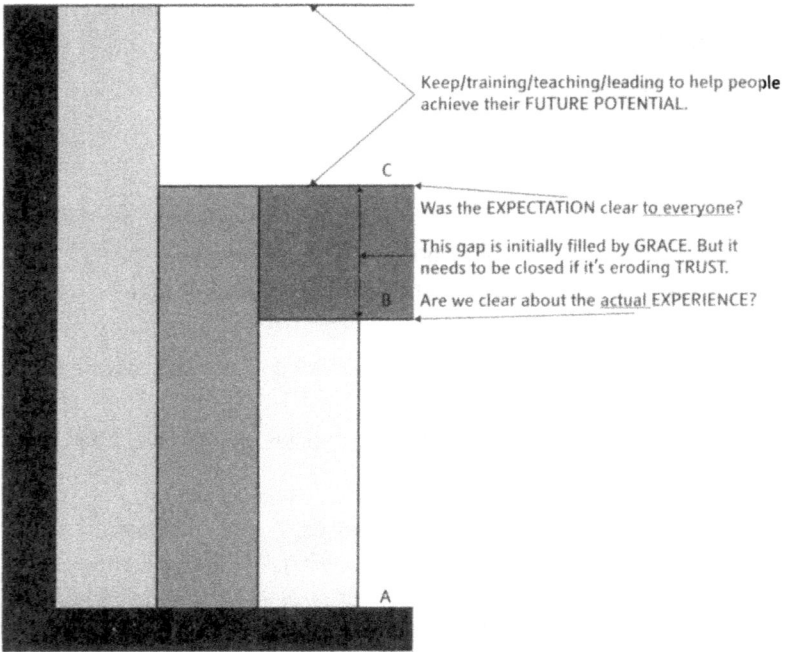

Keep/training/teaching/leading to help people achieve their FUTURE POTENTIAL.

C

Was the EXPECTATION clear to everyone?

This gap is initially filled by GRACE. But it needs to be closed if it's eroding TRUST.

B   Are we clear about the actual EXPERIENCE?

A

Personal Commitment to "Rules of Engagement"

☐ I agree to make the commitment to choose TRUST and to be TRUSTWORTHY.

_____   ____/____/____

Team Member   *Date*

APPENDIX 9
Board Survey

**Prepared by William C. Crothers, founding director
Presidential Leadership Associates**

NAME _____

I am serving as consultant/evaluator for a board development session. Your perceptions and opinions can be helpful and will be kept confidential but will be used to help form a basis for generalized observations. Please rate each statement as (1) strongly agree, (2) agree, (3) disagree, (4) strongly disagree. Then please make comments for each statement. Return the completed questionnaire to Dr. Crothers before _____.

A. Institutional Agenda

1. The Board of Trustees ensures that the mission of the institution is clearly stated and understood both on and off campus.

   1 2 3 4

   How can this be done better?

2. The board has a clear understanding of the distinctive nature of a Christian comprehensive college, as opposed to the perspective of a Bible college, a liberal arts college, or a secular university?

   1 2 3 4

   Comments.

B. Board/President Relation

1. The board has delegated appropriate responsibility and authority to the president and properly distinguished between its role in policy formation and the president's role in administration.

   1 2 3 4

   Comments.

2. There is a climate of mutual trust and support between the board and the president.   1 2 3 4
How do you know?

3. The board takes direct ownership of policy development and governance for the college.   1 2 3 4

4. The board openly champions the current institutional direction and vision as advocated by the president.   1 2 3 4

5. The president is keeping the board informed on issues the college is facing.   1 2 3 4

C. Board Organization and Functioning

1. The board is organized and operated such that it is effective, has a high-level participation, and engenders confidence from its constituencies.   1 2 3 4
Comments.

2. The board has a committee that assesses the performance of individual members, including their financial support, before their membership is renewed for another term.   1 2 3 4

3. Although the board members come from different constituencies (alumni, church, community, etc.), they do exercise independence in thought and action in the interest of the college. They do recognize the distinctive roles of the church and the college.   1 2 3 4
Comments.

4. The board respects the traditions of American higher education, such as separate roles of administration and faculty, importance of research as well as teaching, academic freedom, and the consultative process in decision-making.   1 2 3 4
Comments.

5. The board invests considerable time in strategic planning.

    1 2 3 4

    In what way is it involved?

6. The board is composed of a sufficient range of expertise, perspectives, and external relationships to allow it to significantly
   develop the institution.   1 2 3 4
   Comments.

7. The board has approved a campus master plan and monitors
   the maintenance programs sufficiently to be assured that they
   are not deferred to the detriment of the campus.   1 2 3 4

8. The board takes leadership responsibility for fund-raising for
   the college with many engaging at a personal level. 1 2 3 4

9. The board oversees the financial affairs of the campus and
   assumes responsibility to assure that sufficient resources are
   available to fulfill the mission.   1 2 3 4
   How can the board improve in this function?

10. The board monitors the risk management of the organization.

    1 2 3 4

11. The board should alter its policies and practices with regard to
    the following:
    a. Size   1 2 3 4
    b. Length of term   1 2 3 4
    c. Numbers of successive terms (term limits) 1 2 3 4
    d. Age limit   1 2 3 4
    e. Gender composition   1 2 3 4
    f. Minority composition   1 2 3 4
    g. Geographic composition   1 2 3 4
    h. Attendance record   1 2 3 4
    i. Criteria for membership   1 2 3 4

12. Meeting agendas tend to:
    a. Focus on policy issues and the big picture.   1 2 3 4
    b. Include all necessary supporting information.   1 2 3 4
    c. Be received in a timely manner.   1 2 3 4

13. Board meetings are of sufficient duration and frequency to appropriately do the business of the board.   1 2 3 4

14. The committee structure and function:
    a. Facilitates the work of the board efficiently.   1 2 3 4
    b. Gives the full board the opportunity to consider adequately all important matters.   1 2 3 4
    c. Only recommends to the full board, requiring the full board to take action on all committee action.   1 2 3 4

D. General

1. What are the major strengths of the board?

2. What are the major concerns about the board?

3. What three things should the board focus on for the next three years?

Action Plan for Local Innovation

Phase One: Informational Constituency Presentation (congregation, church board, or the organization responsible for leading the change)

- Address the churchmanship issue. (We should be committed to the church whether or not our opinions are chosen. The goal is to help the congregation be truly committed to the church before the decision concerning the change is made. This can produce an atmosphere of trust. And it is only in this atmosphere of trust that the issue can be honestly explored and discussed.)
- Present the problem being addressed by the change.
- Present rationale for the proposed change. (Tie it to the mission of the church.)
- Use visuals if appropriate. Let them see what the change would look like.
- Imagine what the future might be like if the change does not occur. What is the cost of not changing?
- Ask people who would like to respond to the issue to do so in writing *(this would include both those in favor and those who are opposed)*. Parameters for responding should be given (one page, typed, address the issues, no personal attacks on people will be read, no anonymous responses, and so on).

Phase Two: Response Presentation to the Leadership (team making the decision)

- The task force gathers the responses and presents them to the leadership (church board or the team charged with making the decision).
- Dialogue about the responses:
  Which ones are informative?
  Which ones are just emotional but irrational?

What changes need to be made to the change proposal to make it better?

What issues need to be addressed with the congregation in light of the responses?

Phase Three: Second Constituency Presentation
- Let them know the team has reviewed and considered the responses.
- Address the pertinent issues raised. (Remind them of the cost of not changing.)
- Inform of changes and the *final* proposed change.
- Option: If the situation is very explosive, utilize a point/counter-point format. (Present the written objection and then the written response.) Also address any issue that may have been overlooked earlier.
- Phase One and Two may need to be repeated, depending on the issues raised.

Phase Four: Straw Poll/Survey
Insert a survey in the bulletin on Sunday morning (or Survey Monkey) giving a wide range of responses. Example:
- ☐ I am in total agreement with the proposed change.
- ☐ I believe the proposed change to be a good idea.
- ☐ It doesn't matter to me.
- ☐ I believe a change is needed, but not this particular solution (suggestion: _____).
- ☐ I do not support the proposed change but will support the will of the majority.
- ☐ I do not support the proposed change and will leave this church if it is adopted.

Phase Five: Final Decision by the Leadership Team—Pass or Defeat.

Phase Six: Assurance—Assure the people that the change will be reevaluated after a sufficient time period for success.
Goals:
- Response needs to be measurable rather than just emotional.
- Use visuals.
- Leave the room for various outcomes.

- Create a common base of understanding and purpose.
- Promote constructive dialogue.
- Promote Christian responses.

Note: Any manual requirements for change should be followed.

Note: In developing your plan for initiating change, a time line should also be developed.

Moving College Governance from Good to Great

1. Great institutions have Great Boards. Great Boards require board-oriented presidents. These boards and presidents do not compete, but have separate, complementary roles and function as partners in a trust relationship.

2. A Great Board adopts a powerful God-honoring mission which leads to changed lives, articulates the values and strategies to accomplish that mission, agrees on the major strategic goals, then identifies how to monitor/assess progress, changing as necessary.

3. A Great Board selects a president who is equipped to advance the mission within board policy parameters. Then the board governs in ways that support, fairly compensate, annually evaluate and, if necessary, terminate the president, always with the best interests of the college or university in mind.

4. A Great Board elects a chair who is able and willing to manage the board to maintain the integrity of the structure, process and protocols which the whole board has determined is best, leaving campus administration to the president who leads within board policies.

5. A Great Board defines the criteria for trustees, then selects, orients, trains, evaluates and rewards board service for those who collectively set board policies and, individually, give time, talent and treasure to the institution as volunteers totally committed to its mission.

6. A Great Board welcomes administration's input in formulating policies that the board adopts and documents in an organized, written Board Policies Manual of 15-20 pages, plus a few attachments, which is improved at every meeting as the board learns and adjusts based on monitoring data it defines and expects from the administration.

7. A Great Board often organizes itself into committees or task forces, which speak to the board, not for the board and which do board-related work rather than oversee or advise administrators on their work. Policy recommendations are their end product.

8. A Great Board insists on great meetings that include relevant information in advance, time for fellowship and learning, and agendas focused on improving board policies. Oral reports are limited in order to allow 20-30% of the plenary meeting times for board dialogue among the trustees on significant issues.

9. A Great Board insists on accountability through observance of the law; legal, financial and program audits; avoidance of conflicts of interest; adherence to board protocols; evaluation of the board as a whole and of individual trustees; and appropriate transparency with its stakeholders.

10. A Great Board is intentional in the pursuit of excellence. Trustees are forward-looking, always learning more about higher education, focusing on outcomes/results. They discipline themselves and they change. They recognize, appreciate, and enjoy the process of governance!

Robert C. Andringa, Ph.D.
From *Good Governance Toolbox,* <www.TheAndringaGroup.com>. Used by permission.